COPYRIGHT EDITION.

THE

Army of the Potomac:

ITS

ORGANIZATION, ITS COMMANDER,

AND

ITS CAMPAIGN.

BY

THE PRINCE DE JOINVILLE.

Translated from the French,

WITH NOTES,

BY WILLIAM HENRY HURLBERT.

NEW YORK:
ANSON D. F. RANDOLPH,
No. 683 BROADWAY.
1862.

Edward O. Jenkins, Printer, 20 North William Street, N. Y.

COPYRIGHT EDITION.

THE

Army of the Potomac:

ITS

ORGANIZATION, ITS COMMANDER,

AND

ITS CAMPAIGN.

BY

THE PRINCE DE JOINVILLE.

Translated from the French,

WITH NOTES,

BY WILLIAM HENRY HURLBERT.

NEW YORK:
ANSON D. F. RANDOLPH,
No. 683 BROADWAY.
1862.

EDWARD O. JENKINS,
Printer and Stereotyper,
No. 20 North William St.

The article of which the following pages are a translation appeared in the number of the *Revue des Deux Mondes* for October 15th, 1862. It is there entitled "Campagne de l'Armèe du Potomac, Mars–Juillet, 1862," and bears the signature of "A. Trognon." It is well understood in Paris that this signature is the *nom de plume* of one of the princes of the House of Orleans, and from the internal evidence afforded by the paper itself I have been led to believe that it was probably written by the Prince de Joinville, who accompanied his nephews, the Comte de Paris and the Duc de Chartres, throughout the period of their service in the Army of the Union, and that it was composed upon the data furnished by the journals of one or both of those princes, collated with his own observations and recollections. I have accordingly accepted the well-authenticated rumor which ascribes its authorship to him. I have also taken the liberty of affixing to the translation a title which more fully describes the scope and nature of the paper. As the reader will perceive, it is a critical and historical sketch of the rise, progress, character and fortunes of the army which was assembled at Washington for the invasion of Virginia, from the time of its first organization in 1861, down to the end of the campaign before Richmond in 1862.

It is written with the freedom and force of an accomplished military man, anxious to do justice to the merits and to point out the defects of an army which he has studied in the camp and in the field; master of his subject; temperate in tone, and in style equally free from the carelessness of the amateur, and the pedantry of the professional soldier.

Recent events have given a peculiar importance to the facts here presented, and it will not be easy for any candid person to read these pages without feeling that the causes of the military misfortunes which will make the year 1862 so painfully remarkable in our history demand the fullest and most searching investigation.

The failure of the Army of the Potomac to achieve either of the grand immediate objects which it moved from before Washington in March to effect, the dispersion, namely, of the main confederate army under General Johnston and the occupation of Richmond, has been variously attributed:

1. To the constitutional unfitness of General McClellan for the conduct of operations requiring boldness in the conception and decision in the execution.

2. To the presumed bias of that commander's political opinions. Those who adopt this theory of the origin of our reverses, charge upon General McClellan that he has always sought to avoid driving the insurgent States to the wall, in the belief that the soothing influence of time and the blockade would eventually bring them to accept terms of reconciliation and reunion.

3. To the constant interference of an "Aulic Council" at Washington with the plans of our commanders in the field, an interference which when it does not positively interrupt the progress of operations actually begun, by depriving a general of some portion of the force on which his calculations were based, must still greatly cripple his efficiency by making it incompatible with common prudence for him to take serious risks and essay adventurous combinations.

4. To the superior military abilities of the Southern commanders enabling them to outmanœuvre our leaders and to accumulate overwhelming forces upon the separate armies of an array in the aggregate greatly outnumbering their own.

The testimony under these different heads of the Prince de Joinville may be thus summed up:

1. The Prince de Joinville testifies that General McClellan's original plan of campaign was in the highest degree direct and aggressive.

This plan was formed at a time when the command of the waters of Virginia was entirely in our hands, and it involved so rapid a concentration of the federal forces at a point within striking distance of Richmond as must have been followed either by the evacuation of that city or by a decisive action in the field. He testifies also that when by the sudden and formidable advent of the Merrimac and by the retreat of Johnston from Manassas upon Richmond and Yorktown, this original plan was made impracticable, General McClellan conceived a second plan for turning the position at Yorktown, which was also direct and aggressive in its character, and which was made impracticable by the sudden withdrawal of the *corps d'armeé* necessary to its execution.

In respect to the operations of McClellan before Richmond, he testifies that it was the intention of that general to follow up his arrival upon the Chickahominy by an immediate assault in combination with the army of McDowell, and that this intention was defeated by the complete separation of that army from his own in consequence of orders sent to McDowell from Washington. He gives it as his opinion, however, that greater activity and more rapid aggressive movements on the part of General McClellan during the months of May and June and at the battle of Fair Oaks, might possibly have resulted in the fall of Richmond, but this opinion he qualifies by intimating that the disposition of the General to instant action was curbed and dampened during that time by the influence of the checks previously imposed upon the development of his strategy; and he ascribes the final extrication of the Army of the Potomac from a position which had become untenable, to a movement in an extraordinary degree decisive and audacious.

2. Writing after a familiar intercourse of months with the General-in-Chief of the army, in which he must necessarily have imbibed his leading views in respect to national policy, the Prince's language makes it more than probable that General McClellan earnestly believed a prompt and decisive victory over the confederate army to be the surest if not the only means of securing the restoration of the Union, and that so believing, he thought it essential that a conciliatory temper towards the Southern people should precede, accompany and succeed the victory of the sword.

3. The Prince de Joinville asserts distinctly that the interference of the Government with the plans of General McClellan was constant, embarrassing, and of such a nature as finally to make it next to impossible for that General to risk the safety of the army under his charge in any extensive operation the success of which was not substantially assured in advance.

4. The Prince's account of the retreat of McClellan from Richmond shows that he considers the confederate Generals to have been completely out-manœuvred and out-witted at that time by their adversary, whose concentration they did not comprehend in time to prevent it, and whose escape they were not able to intercept although superior to him in numbers and in knowledge of the country, fighting within sight of their base, and supported by the active good will of a whole population.

So runs the evidence upon these four points of a witness whose competency and impartiality we have certainly no right or reason to impeach. He may have been misinformed; uninformed, the responsibility which he assumes in publishing his narrative forbids us to suppose he can have been.

Until the publication of authentic official documents, the paper here submitted to the reader must be considered to be the fullest and fairest story of the great Campaign of 1862 yet given to the world. As such it should receive the most serious attention. The reputation of any one man or set of men is a slight thing in comparison with the success or failure of the nation in a war of life and death. If the Prince de Joinville's statements can be proved incorrect and his inferences unsound; if General McClellan be really responsible by reason of his military incapacity or his political theories for our great disappointments, then it will be much for the nation to forgive him the past and forget him in the future.

If the Prince's statements be proved correct and his inferences sound, they must be regarded as a substantial indictment of the Administration in respect to its management of the war; and the removal of General McClellan from the command of his army in the field must be pronounced a sign of evil omen on which too much stress can hardly be laid.

I believe the present translation, although rapidly made, will not be found inaccurate. I have ventured to append to it a few notes upon subjects connected with the condition of things at the South, in respect to which I had reason to believe myself more fully and correctly informed than the circumstances of the author permitted him to be.

W. H. H.

New York, Nov. 15, 1862.

Note.—Since the first edition of this translation was issued, I have received authority from Brigadier-General Barry, Chief of Artillery of the Army of the Potomac, to correct the writer's statement in regard to the loss of guns on the retreat from Richmond (p. 93). Instead of three, the army lost but one siege-gun, an 8-inch howitzer, the carriage of which broke down. No feature of this extraordinary retreat reflects higher credit upon the army than this brilliant achievement of the artillery service and its chief; and as the most extravagant falsehoods upon this point have obtained credence and circulation abroad, I take a particular pleasure in here recording the truth, confident that no man out of America will more heartily rejoice in it than the author whom I am thus enabled to set right.

THE ARMY OF THE POTOMAC.

Military events succeed each other rapidly in America, and the public follows them with an attention which is all the more anxious that it does not always understand them, partly through lack of knowledge of the organization of American armies and of the character of their commanders and their soldiers; but above all, through the difficulty of getting at the impressions of persons who, being competent to observe these memorable struggles, actually took part in them themselves.

The pages here offered to the reader, will perhaps meet this legitimate public curiosity. They are the sum and setting forth of the notes of an officer, who took part in the last battles in Virginia, and who has never ceased to watch and follow up the grand operations of the war, in respect to which, he will, no doubt, give us new details; our duty is simply to gather up and group the impressions and the recollections scattered through the numerous letters, and the private journal of the officer in question.

I.

The Creation of the Army.

On my arrival in America, the curtain had just fallen on the first act of the secessionist insurrection. The attack on Fort Sumter by the people of Charleston, had been the prologue, then came the disaster of Bull Run. The army of the

South was encamped within sight of Washington. Works of defence were hastily thrown up around that Capital. The roar of the cannon was heard from time to time along the front of the line. Amid these commotions the army of the Potomac came into being.

Up to this time, the Federal Government, taken by surprise, had only hit in haste upon certain provisional measures which aggravated instead of dissipating the danger. All the advantages, at the outset of the insurrection, were with the insurgents. They were ready for an armed conflict, the North was not. In truth the work of secession had been long preparing. Under the pretext of a military organization to repress slave insurrections, the States of the South had created a permanent militia, ready to march at the first signal. Special schools had been founded in which the sons of the Slaveholders imbibed the inspiration of those good and bad qualities which combine to form a race of soldiers. Meanwhile, the northern man, reposing with confidence upon the regular operation of the Constitution, remained absorbed in his own affairs behind his counter. The national army of the Union belonged almost entirely to the men of the South. For many years the Federal power had been in their hands, and they had not failed to fill, with creatures of their own, all the departments of its administration, and especially the war office and the army. Mr. Jefferson Davis, long Secretary at War, had done more to accomplish this than any other single man.

The disposition of the northern people facilitated his task. Among the laborious and still somewhat puritanical populations of New England, the career of arms was looked upon as that of an idler. The West Point Academy enjoyed no great consideration in that part of the country, and the heads of families were by no means anxious to send their sons to it. Finally, on the eve of the crisis which was to follow Mr. Lincoln's election, Mr. Floyd, now a General among the secessionists and then war Secretary under Mr. Buchanan, had taken pains to send to the South the contents of all the Federal arsenals, and to despatch the whole of the regular army to Texas, putting between the army and Washington the barrier of the slave States, in order to paralyze the sentiment of duty which might lead the soldiers to follow that small number among their officers who should remain loyal to their flag. Nothing accordingly was lacking in the precautions taken by the Confederacy. They had dealt with the navy as with the army. It was dispersed at the four corners of the globe.

As to the North, it did just nothing. Yet it had not wanted warnings. For many years Secession had been openly preached. A curious book called the "Partisan Leader," published twenty years ago, is a proof of this. Under the form of a novel this book is a really prophetic picture of the war which is at this moment desolating Virginia, a picture so highly colored as easily to explain the ardor with which the imagination of the Creole ladies has espoused the cause of the South. But it was believed in the North, as in various other places, that "all would come right." The North felt itself the stronger, and saw no reason for troubling itself prematurely. It was the old story of the hare and the tortoise. Moreover, in the last resort, the North counted on the several hundred thousand volunteers set down in the almanacks as representing the military force of the country, and supposed by the popular mind to be irresistible. The North was quickly undeceived. The people of the South were beaten in the presidential election. They were still masters of the Senate, and it was not the loss of power which roused them, it was the wound inflicted on their pride. This was used by the ambitious managers of the party of Secession to excite the Southern mind, and the standard of the insurrection was raised. The federal power, still passive, allowed the period for compromise, the period for conciliation, and the period for energetic and instantaneous repression to roll by alike unimproved. On both sides the States begin to arm for the inevitable strife; but the South has the warriors, the arms, the organization, the will and the passion. The North is impotent even to provision Fort Sumter, and the volunteers raised for three months, as if that was to be the limit of the campaign, get themselves beaten at Bull Run, not through want of courage, for the instances of individual valor were numerous; nor yet through the fault of General McDowell, who commanded them, and whose plans deserved success, but through the absence of organization and of discipline.

After Bull Run there was no room left for illusions. A great war was before the country. Intoxicated with pride, encouraged by all those who for one or another reason wished ill to the United States, the South it was plain would never again consent to return to the Union until it should have suffered severe reverses.

The hopes of its ambitious leaders were more than realized. They had struck a successful vein, and nothing could make them abandon it. At the North, on the other hand, humiliation had opened all men's eyes. It was felt that, having on their side, with the superiority of population and wealth, the right and the legality of the question—having the sacred trust of the Constitution to defend against a factious minority, which after all, only took up arms to extend slavery—they would become a by-word for the world if they did not resist. They felt, besides, that if the doctrine of secession were once admitted and sanctioned, it would be susceptible of infinite application; that, from one rupture to another, it would bring about a chaos which must very soon open the way to despotism. They felt, in short, that it was chimerical to suppose that two Powers could live side by side in peace who had not yet made real trial of their respective strength—who were separated radically, notwithstanding their common tongue and origin, by the institution of slavery—the one wishing its development and the other its abolition—who were separated, also, by interests which no Custom House line could conciliate, and by the impossibility of regulating, without daily quarrels, the numerous questions connected with the navigation of the Western rivers. All these reasons, obvious to every mind, added to the pain of wounded self-love, and to the novelty of a warlike movement in that land of peace, resulted in setting on foot the immense armament with which the Northern States have up to this day sustained the war against the powerful efforts of Secession.

Let us pause here before passing on to the numerous criticisms that we shall have to make, to admire the energy, the devotion, the spirit of courageous self-denial with which the population of those States—rather leading the Government than led by it—has of itself, and under the single impulse of its patriotic good sense, given uncounted men and money, sacrificed its comforts, renounced voluntarily and for the public good, its tastes, its habits, even to the freedom of the press, and that, too, not under the influence of a momentary passion, not in a transport of transient enthusiasm, but coolly and for a distant object—that of national greatness.

The North went seriously to work to create an army—a grand army. Seconded by public opinion, Congress resolved upon the raising of five hundred thousand men, with the funds necessary for the purpose. Unfortunately it could not command the traditions, the training and the experience requisite to form and manage such a military force. It was able to collect masses of men and immense material, as if by enchantment; but it had not the power to create by a vote the spirit of discipline, of obedience, and that hierarchical respect, without which there may be armed crowds, but there can be no army. Here is the reef upon which many generous efforts have been dashed to pieces. Here is an original vice whose fatal influence we shall everywhere encounter. We shall discover the germ of this vice by a rapid examination of the machinery which was used to improvise this first creation.

According to American law the Federal Government maintains, in time of peace, a permanent regular army. It may, besides, in cases of necessity, war or insurrection, call to its standard as many regiments of volunteers as it may deem expedient. The regular army, formed by recruiting only, numbered 20,000 men before the secession. The officers, educated exclusively at the military school, were remarkable. Well educated, versed practically in their profession, understanding the necessity of absolute command, they maintained in their small force the most vigorous discipline. This was an excellent nucleus for an army, but the rebellion, as I have before remarked, had brought on its dissolution. The greater part of the officers—more than three hundred—passed over to the South. The soldiers—all Irish or German—lost in the solitudes of Texas, were dispersed. From two to three thousand men, at most, returned from California or Utah to take part in the war. This was chiefly important as bringing back a certain number of officers who might preside over the organization—such as it was—of the army of volunteers about to be raised. In Europe, where we have learned to recognize the comparative value of the regular soldier, and of this costly and capricious amateur soldier, who is called a volunteer, the loss of the aid of the regular army, small as it was, would have brought us to despair, and we should have set to work to increase the army by enlarging its organization and incorporating recruits. An army of sixty thousand regulars would have done more than double or triple the number of volunteers; but in America they do not know this, and besides, they do not wish to know it. It would involve a renunciation of the general and deeply rooted creed, that every American, when he wishes to do a thing, may find within himself, without any apprenticeship, the power to do it; and, consequently, there is no volunteer who, when he puts on the uniform, does not at the same time put on the qualities of a soldier. Add to this that the West Point officers, simply from the fact that they have received a superior education, and recognize the necessity of a hierarchy, are regarded as aristocrats, and everything aristocratic is bad. Such officers were safe with the mercenaries who consented to obey them, and under their orders to keep the peace against the frontier tribes of Indians; but to place under their command a great army, which must be reduced to the subordination of the camps, was to run the risk of grave political dangers. An eighteenth Brumaire is not to be made with volunteers. Therefore, everything having to be created, it was decided to create an army of volunteers—an ephemeral army, comparatively inefficient, and, above all, ruinously expensive. The American volunteer is richly paid. His pay is $13—more than 65 francs—per month. Besides that, an allowance of $8 per month is paid to his wife in his absence; and this, it may be said in passing, has brought about many sudden marriages at the moment of departure for the army. Ordinarily there are no deductions from his pay for clothing or other supplies. The volunteer is provided with everything, and is supplied so liberally with rations that he daily throws away a part of them. One may imagine what such an army must cost. This would not matter if even at such an expense the country were well served. It is not so, however. It is ill served for want of discipline, not that the military laws and regulations were not severe enough; but they were not enforced, and could not be, in consequence of the primary organization of the regiment, and of the composition of its corps of officers. And here we come to the essential vice of an American army.

How is a regiment of volunteers actually formed? As soon as Congress has voted the number of men, they calculate at Washington the quota which each State must furnish, according to its resources and population. This calculation being made, each Governor announces that there are to be so many regiments raised within the limits of his jurisdiction. The regiment of one battalion only, is the American military unit. Affairs are managed in this way:

Persons present themselves offering to raise a regiment. Each sets forth his claims, his influence in the State, or among a certain portion of the population, which will enable him to procure easily the necessary number of men, his devotion to the party in power, etc. From among the persons thus presented the Governor makes his choice. Generally the person upon whom the choice falls has laid it down as a condition precedent that he shall have the command of the regiment; and thus Mr. So-and-So, a lawyer or a doctor, never having handled a sword, but feeling within himself an improvised vocation, becomes a colonel at the start, and puts himself in connection with all the recruiting agencies and with all the furnishers of equipment and clothing supplies for the future regiment. The next thing is to find the soldiers; this is not so easy, for there is a great deal of rivalry. They apply to all their comrades, traverse the country, and resort to various plans. This is done quickly and well in America, for the Americans have an inventive mind. Most frequently they find friends who, seized with the same martial ardor, promise to bring so many recruits if they be made—the one captain, the other lieutenant, another sergeant, and so forth. The framework is formed and is partly filled up; it only remains to complete it. It is then that recourse is had to extraordinary measures—to those gigantic posters which set forth in pompous terms all the advantages to be gained by joining the corps. They go among the Catholic priests to procure Irishmen, and give the coveted privilege of sutlership to the individual who promises the necessary complement of men. Thus the regiment finds itself organized, and the lists are carried to the Governor, who approves everything. The regiment is mustered, clothed and equipped, and forwarded by railroad to the seat of war. Sometimes, even frequently, the grades are made to depend on election; but that is generally only a formality, as everything has been arranged beforehand by those interested.

The inconveniences of this system are obvious. The officers, from the colonel down to the lowest in rank, do not know the first word of the military art, and if they have any real aptitude for it and any warlike qualities, these are still to be proved. The soldiers have no illusions on this point. "They know no more about it than we do, we are well acquainted with them," they say of those who command them. Hence, there is no superiority of knowledge on the part of the officer over the soldier, and no superiority of social position in a country where no such superiority is recognized. Most frequently, also, it is with an idea of being a candidate for political office that the officer has taken up arms. It is to make himself a name in the eyes of the voters. And these future voters are the soldiers. What would become of the popularity he expects to enjoy if he were rough to the soldiers, or showed himself too exacting in the service? All these causes bring about the want of authority with officers, and the want of respect among soldiers. Of course, then, there can be neither hierarchy nor discipline. All this has been ameliorated by force of necessity, and in the school of experience. Even from the beginning there were exceptions to it; some colonels, impelled by a real vocation, or animated by an ardent patriotism, succeeded in overcoming the obstacles placed in their path. Sometimes an officer of the regular army, desirous of distinguishing himself, and having influence enough in his State, raised a regiment and obtained from it an admirable result.

Thus, a young lieutenant of engineers, named Warren, was marvellously successful with the Fifth New York regiment, of which he was colonel. This regiment served as engineers and artillery at the siege of Yorktown, and, having again become infantry, conducted itself like the most veteran troops at the battles of the Chickahominy, where it lost half of its force. And yet these were volunteers—but they felt the knowledge and superiority of their chief. Generally, however, the chief is simply a comrade who wears a different costume. He is obeyed in every day routine, but voluntarily. In the same way the soldiers don't trouble themselves about him when circumstances become serious. From the point of view of American equality, there is no good reason to obey him. Besides, in the eyes of the greater number this title of volunteer does not signify the soldier who devotes himself generously and voluntarily to save the country or to acquire glory, but rather the well-paid soldier, who only does what he wishes and pleases. This is so true that, although the pay and time of service are the same for volunteers and regulars, the recruiting of regulars has become almost impossible. All that class of men who enlisted when regulars alone existed, from a taste for camp life, now join the volunteers. On one side is license, on the other discipline—the choice is easily made. The habits created by universal suffrage also play their part and are reproduced on the field of battle. By a tacit agreement the regiment marches against the enemy, advances under fire and begins to deliver its volleys; the men are brave, very brave; they are killed and wounded in great numbers, and then, when by a tacit agreement they think they have done enough for military honor, they all march off together. The colonel perhaps attempts to give a direction, an impulse, but generally his efforts are in vain. As to the officers, they never think of it. Why should they attempt it, and why should they be obeyed if the majority of the regiment has made up its mind to retreat? Obedience in such an army is like the obedience which children playing at soldiers render to him among their comrades whom they have made their captain. Is any argument necessary to show the inconvenience of such a state of things? Nevertheless, the Government put its hand on an immense mass of armed men, a multitude of regiments; for the country had responded unanimously and vigorously to the call for volunteers. Never, we believe, has any nation created, of herself, by her own will, by her single resources, without coercion of any kind, without government pressure, and in such a short space of time, so considerable an armament. Free governments, whatever may be their faults and the excesses to which they may give rise, always preserve an elasticity and creative power which nothing can equal. Only, the vices of organization which we have pointed out singularly impaired the value of this military gathering.

It was to remedy these vices as far as possible that General McClellan and old officers of West Point, who had become, by force of circumstances, generals of brigade or of division, devoted all their efforts. Regiments were brigaded by fours, and brigades divisioned by threes. To each division four batteries were given, three of them served by volunteers and one by regulars. The latter was to serve as a model for the others, and its captain took command of all the artillery of the division. At one time they had some idea of placing a battalion of regulars in each division of volunteers, to act the part of "lance head," which Lord Clyde attributes to the European troops in the Sepoy armies; but the idea was abandoned. It appeared wiser to keep together the only

2

really disciplined troops that they possessed; besides, as it was made, the divisional formation was a good one, and has been of very great utility. It next became necessary to provide for the administrative services for provisions, munitions and transports, and to organize artillery reserves, the engineer corps, the pontoon corps, the topographical brigade, the telegraphs and the hospitals.

This prodigious labor was accomplished with a rapidity and a success which are extraordinary, when we think that the whole thing had to be achieved without any assistance from the past. Not only was there nobody to be found who knew anything, except from books, of the management of the numerous threads by which an army is held together and moved; not only was the country destitute of all precedents in the matter; the number even of those who had travelled in Europe and seen for themselves what a grand collection of troops is, was infinitely small. The American army had no traditions but those of the Mexican campaign of General Scott—a brilliant campaign, in which there were many difficulties to be overcome, but which presented nothing like the gigantic proportions of the present war. Moreover, in Mexico General Scott had with him the entire regular army, and here there only remained its feeble ruins. In Mexico the regulars were the main body, the volunteers were only the accessory, and, as it were, the ornament. The old general, who was one day asked what he then did to maintain discipline in their ranks, answered, "Oh, they knew that if they straggled off they would be massacred by the guerrillas." The two cases, therefore, had nothing in common, and the management of these great armies of volunteers, in spite of all the efforts to regularize them, was a problem which offered many unknown data.

At the South the organization of the insurrectionary forces presented fewer difficulties. The revolutionary government had quickly assumed in the hands of Mr. Jefferson Davis the dictatorial form. Sustained by an Oligarchy of three hundred thousand slaveholders, of whom he was the choice, and whose violent passions he personified, Mr. Davis had set himself actively at work to create an army fit to contend against the formidable preparations of the federal government. A former pupil of West Point, a former General of volunteers in Mexico, a former Secretary of War in the Union, he had all the requisite conditions to perform his task well. He applied to it his rare capacity. He was seconded by the flower of the former federal staff, by the more military spirit of the Southerners, and also by the assistance of all the adventurers, filibusters and others, whom the South had always nurtured in view of those continual invasions to which slavery condemns her. I have no idea of drawing here a sketch of the separatist army; but I wish to point out two important differences which mark its organization as compared with that of the North. The officers were chosen and nominated directly by the President, and were sent with the regiments to fill their positions. There was no comradeship between them and the soldiers. The soldiers did not know them, and therefore regarded them as their superiors. They were not men who were subsequently, in private life, to find themselves again their equals. In short these officers belonged to that class of slave owners who living by the labor of their inferiors and accustomed to command them, attached to the soil by the hereditary transmission of the paternal estate and of the black serfs who people it, possess to a certain extent, the qualities of aristocrats. In their hands the discipline of the army could not suffer. Numerous shootings caused discipline to be respected, and on the day of battle they led their soldiers valiantly, and were valiantly followed. In the second place, Mr. Davis quickly perceived that the volunteer system would be powerless to furnish him with enough men to sustain the fratricidal strife into which he had plunged his country. He came rapidly to conscription, to forced recruiting. It was no longer a contract between the soldier and his colonel, or between the soldier and the State, which would still leave a possibility of its being annulled, and which brought with it absolute obligations. It was the law, the authority, the power of the State, which carried off all able-bodied men and made them march up blindly to what was called the defence of their country. There was no hesitation possible. Bound by the obligation of duty, the soldier became at once more submissive and more reconciled to the sacrifice. In the situation in which the South was, these measures were wise, and there is no doubt that they contributed at the beginning of the war to secure great advantages to its army. Nevertheless, we are far from reproaching Mr. Lincoln for not having recourse to such violent measures. The leaders of an insurrection recognize no obstacle, and are stopped by no scruples when the object is to assure the triumph of their ambitious views, and particularly to escape the consequences of defeat. They recoil before nothing, and have no repugnance to revolutionary expedients; but Mr. Lincoln and his advisers were the legitimate representatives of the nation, and if it fell to them to suppress a revolt, they did not wish, unless in case of absolute necessity, to touch the guarantees which, up to that time, had made the American people the happiest and freest people of the earth.

II.

Plans of the Campaign.

The army once improvised, it next became necessary to decide how to employ it—in other words, to choose the plan of the campaign. The general plan was simple. The idea of conquering and occupying a territory so vast as that of the

Confederate States could not even be considered; but for the purpose of escaping the dangers, actual and possible, of such a formidable insurrection, it was necessary to attain three results: to blockade efficiently the insurgent coast; to get control of the Mississippi river, and of the entire system of Western waters; and, finally, to drive the rebel government out Richmond, its capital. By the blockade the rebels are isolated from the foreigners whose sympathy had been promised them; the introduction of powder and firearms is prevented; exportation, and the resources which it might have procured, are stopped; and, finally, the introduction of supplies from abroad is guarded against, which would, in spite of the state of war, have penetrated into the North, to the great detriment of national manufactures and of the Federal treasury. To the navy belonged the duty of this blockade. It discharged that duty rather inefficiently at first for want of sufficient means; but by degrees the surveillance grew closer and closer until it became difficult to evade it.

The possession of the Mississippi was an imperious necessity. The great river and its affluents are the outlets of all the countries which they water. They are the arteries of the Western States—States which have, up to this time, remained faithful to the Union, but in which their material interests might at length chill their enthusiasm, and speak even louder than their convictions. To restore the Union as a matter of interest, on the basis of slavery, has been for a long time past the programme of the Southern leaders. To abandon to them without a struggle the Western rivers would be to concede half the question. It was therefore decided to bring on a conflict on this theatre. The navy recaptured New Orleans by a brilliant *coup de main*. That was the principal point. The Federals thus put the key in their pocket. As to the course of the Mississippi, the task of reconquering it was confided to the Western armies, admirably seconded by Commodore

Foote's flotilla of iron-clad batteries and steam rams. In those regions the war assumed quite a new character. So long as they were carried on only by water the operations were very rapid. The enemy could not intercept the magnificent navigable highways so favorable to attack which the great rivers of the West supplied. By water Columbus was besieged, whilst by quickly ascending the Tennessee and Cumberland rivers, the communications of the rebel army assigned to the defence of that important post, were cut. Once isolated from its railroads, that army had to retreat southwards. It thus retired from position to position, as fast as the Northern flotilla descended the river, and as the Northern army seized upon the principal railroad branches. The march of the Federals only slackened when, being able to advance no farther by navigable waters, parallel to the Mississippi, such as the Tennessee, they had to reconstruct, as they went along, the railroads necessary for their supplies, which the enemy had destroyed in falling back.

The last operation remained—to drive out of Richmond the insurrectionary government. That government, on being concentrated in the hands of Mr. Davis, took the form of a dictatorship, and thus gave to its seat the importance of a capital. There converge all the great railroad and telegraph lines. Thence, for a year past, have all orders and despatches been dated. To force the Confederate government to abandon that capital would be to inflict upon it an immense check—in the eyes of Europe particularly it would have taken away its prestige. Should this attack have been ventured on as soon as the means supposed to be sufficient were provided, without awaiting the results of the blockade and of the Mississippi campaign? On this question opinions were divided. Some said "yes," arguing thus: that an insurrection should never be given the time to establish itself; that the Federal army, with its defective organization, would be no better in March than in November; that a splendid success on the part of the North, following close upon Bull Run, might finish the war at one blow, by permitting a great effort at conciliation before either side became too much embittered. Others said "no." According to them the great work of reducing the insurrection should be performed on the coast and on the Mississippi. The Richmond campaign, undertaken in the spring, with the Army of the Potomac, made hardier by a winter passed in tents, and recovered from the fatal impressions of Bull Run, would be the *coup de grace* to Secession. The latter course was chosen, either as the result of real deliberation, or of necessity from not having decided in time to act during the fine weather of the autumn of 1861.

And here I may point out, in passing, a characteristic trait of the American people—that is, as well in regard to the people as to an agglomeration of individuals—delay. This delay in resolving and acting, so opposed to the promptitude, the decision, the audacity to which the American, considered as an individual, had accustomed us, is an inexplicable phenomenon which always causes me the greatest astonishment. Is it the abuse of the individual initiative that kills the collective energy? Is it the habit of calculating only on one's self and of acting only for one's self that renders them hesitating and distrustful when they must act with the assistance of others? Is it the never having learned to obey that makes it so difficult to command? Doubtless something of all these causes, and other causes still that escape us, must combine in producing this result, as strange as it is unaccountable; but this delay in action which, besides, appears to belong to the Anglo-Saxon race, is atoned for by a tenacity and a perseverance which failure does not discourage.

Let us, then, leave the federal fleets occupied in blockading the rebel coast, in recapturing New Orleans, in aiding General Halleck to reconquer the course of the Mississippi, and let us follow the career of the Army of the Potomac, destined to engage the great confederate army and to wrest from it, if possible, the possession of the Virginian capital. The winter had passed, for the Northern soldiers, in the work of organization, of drilling, of provisioning; besides, they had constructed around Washington a series of works, of detached forts (to use a well-known expression) which, armed with powerful artillery, would protect the capital from a sudden assault, even though the Army of the Potomac might be absent. The construction of these works furnished scope for thought to those who sought to penetrate the projects of the General; but everything had long been so quiet at Washington that it was only casually that the idea of entering on a campaign presented itself. The enemy still occupied, in great force, his positions of Manassas and Centreville, and for six months past nothing but unimportant skirmishes had occurred between the two armies. Things were in this condition when, on the evening of the 9th of March, one of my friends, tapping me on the shoulder, said: "You don't know the news? The enemy has evacuated Manassas, and the army sets out to-morrow." Next day, in reality, the whole city of Washington was in commotion. A mass of artillery, of cavalry, of wagons, blocked up the streets, moving towards the bridges of the Potomac. On the sidewalks were seen officers bidding tender farewells to weeping ladies. The civilian portion of the population looked coldly on this departure. There was not the least trace of enthusiasm among them. Perhaps this was due to the rain, which was falling in torrents.

On the long bridge, in the midst of several batteries that were laboriously defiling across this bridge which is eternally in ruins, I met General McClellan, on horseback, with an anxious air, riding alone, without aids-de-camp, and escorted only by a few troopers. He who could that day have read the General's soul would have seen there already something of that bitterness which subsequently was to accumulate so cruelly upon him.

Beyond the bridge we found the whole army in motion towards Fairfax Court House, where a great part of it encamped that evening. The cavalry pushed on as far as Centreville and Manassas, which it found abandoned. The enemy was not come up with anywhere; he had had too greatly the start of us. The head-quarters were established as well as possible at Fairfax, a pretty village, with large frame houses standing apart and surrounded by gardens. The population had fled at our approach, almost without an exception. The next day I accompanied a cavalry reconnoissance to Centreville, where I saw the immense barracks which the Confederates had occupied during the winter, and to Manassas, whose smoking ruins left on the mind a deep impression of sadness. On our return we visited the battle field of Bull Run. General McDowell was with us. He could not restrain his tears at the sight of those bleaching bones, which recalled to him so vividly the cruel recollection of his defeat.

While we were making these promenades grave events were occurring in the highest regions of the army. There exists in the American army, as in the English, a commander-in-chief who exercises over the head of all the generals, a supreme authority, regulates the distribution of the troops and directs military operations. These functions, which have been greatly curtailed in the British army, since the Crimean war, were still exercised with all their vigor in America. From the aged General Scott, who had long honorably discharged them, they had passed to General McClellan. We learned on reaching Fairfax, that they had been taken away from him. It is easy to understand the diminution of force and the restrictions upon his usefulness, thus inflicted upon the general-in-chief by a blow in the rear at the very outset of his campaign.

Yet this was but a part of the mischief done him. McClellan

had long known, better than anybody else, the real strength of the rebels at Manassas and Centreville. He was perfectly familiar with the existence of the "wooden cannon" by which it has been pretended that he was kept in awe for six months. But he also knew that till the month of April the roads of Virginia are in such a state that wagons and artillery can only be moved over them by constructing plank roads, a tedious operation, during which the enemy, holding the railways, could either retreat, as he was then actually doing, or move for a blow upon some other point. In any event, had McClellan attacked and carried Centreville, pursuit was impossible and victory would have been barren of results. A single bridge burned would have saved Johnston's whole army. Such are the vast advantages of a railway for a retreating army—advantages which do not exist for the army which pursues it.

We have the right, we think, to say that McClellan never in tended to advance upon Centreville. His long determined pu pose was to make Washington safe by means of a strong garrison, and then to use the great navigable waters and immense naval resources of the North to transport the army by sea to a point near Richmond. For weeks, perhaps for months, this plan had been secretly maturing. Secresy as well as promptness, it will be understood, was indispensable here to success. To keep the secret it had been necessary to confide it to few persons, and hence had arisen one great cause for jealousy of the General.

Be this as it may, as the day of action drew near, those who suspected the General's project, and were angry at not being informed of it; those whom his promotion had excited to envy; his political enemies; (who is without them in America?) in short all those beneath or beside him who wished him ill, broke out into a chorus of accusations of slowness, inaction, incapacity. McClellan, with a patriotic courage which I have always admired, disdained these accusations, and made no reply. He satisfied himself with pursuing his preparations in laborious silence. But the moment came in which, notwithstanding the loyal support given him by the President, that functionary could no longer resist the tempest. A council of war of all the divisional generals was held; a plan of campaign, not that of McClellan, was proposed and discussed. McClellan was then forced to explain his projects, and the *next day they were known to the enemy. Informed no doubt* by one of those thousand female spies who keep up his communications into the domestic circles of the federal enemy, Johnston evacuated Manassas at once. This was a skillful manœuvre. Incapable of assuming the offensive; threatened with attack either at Centreville, where defence would be useless if successful, or at Richmond, the loss of which would be a grave check, and unable to cover both positions at once, Johnston threw his whole force before the latter of the two.

For the Army of the Potomac this was a misfortune. Its movement was unmasked before it had been made. Part of its transports were still frozen up in the Hudson. Such being the state of affairs, was it proper to execute as rapidly as possible the movement upon Richmond by water, or to march upon Richmond by land? Such was the grave question to be settled by the young general in a miserable room of an abandoned house at Fairfax within twenty-four hours. And it was at this moment that the news of his removal as general-in-chief reached him; the news, that is, that he could no longer count upon the co-operation of the other armies of the Union, and that the troops under his own orders were to be divided into four grand *corps* under four separate chiefs named in order of rank, a change which would throw into subaltern positions some young generals of division who had his personal confidence. It is easy to see that here was matter enough to cast a cloud upon the firmest mind. But the General's resolution was promptly taken.

To follow the confederates by land to Richmond at this season of the year was a material impossibility. An incident had just proved this to be so. Gen. Stoneman, with a flying column, had been sent in pursuit of the enemy. This column came up with the enemy on the Rappahannock, along the railway to Gordonsville, and had two engagements with him of no great importance. Then came the rain. The fords were swollen, the bridges carried away, the water-courses could no longer be passed by swimming; they were torrents. Stoneman's column began to suffer for want of provisions, and its situation was perilous. In order to communicate with the army Stoneman had to send two of McClellan's aides-de-camp, who had accompanied him, across a river on a raft of logs tied together with ropes.

Such was the country before the army. Furthermore, the enemy was burning and breaking up all the bridges. Now with the wants of the American soldier and the usual extravagance of his rations, and with the necessity of transporting everything through a country where nothing is to be found, and where the least storm makes the roads impassable, no army can live unless it supports its march upon a navigable water-course or a railway. In Europe our military administration assumes that the transportation service of an army of one hundred thousand men can only provision that army for a three days' march from its base of operations. In America this limit must be reduced to a single day. An American army, therefore, cannot remove itself more than one day's march from the railway or the water-course by which it is supplied; and if the road which it is taking happens to be interrupted by broken bridges it must wait till they are repaired, or move forward without food and without ammunition. I need only add that upon the roads which led to Richmond there were viaducts which it would have required six weeks to reconstruct.

The land march was therefore abandoned and we came back to the movement by water. But this operation also was no longer what it had been when McClellan had conceived it. The revelation of his plans to the enemy had allowed the latter to take his precautions. The evacuation of Manassas had preceded instead of following the opening of the federal campaign. The movement by water could no longer be a surprise. Unfortunately it was now also to lose the advantages of a rapid execution.

A few days had been half lost in a useless pursuit of the enemy while the transports were assembling at Alexandria. At last they were assembled and the order came to embark. But here a new misunderstanding awaited the General. He had been promised transports which could convey 50,000 men at a time. He found vessels hardly equal to the conveyance of half that number. Instead of moving at once, as McClellan had intended, a whole army with its equipage, a number of trips had to be made. The embarkation began March 17. The force consisted of eleven divisions of infantry, 8,000 to 10,000 strong; one division of regulars (inf. and cav.) 6,000 strong; 350 pieces of artillery. The total effective force may have been 120,000 men. At the moment of departure a whole division was detached to form, we know not why, an independent command under General Fremont in the mountains of Virginia. We shall see the Potomac army successively undergo other not less inexplicable diminutions. But we anticipate.

A fortnight was required to move the army to Fortress Monroe. This point was chosen because the apparition of the Merrimac, and her tremendous exhibition of her strength, had made it impossible to regard the federal navy as absolutely mistress of the waters of Virginia.

Fortress Monroe is a regular citadel, built of stone, which occupies the southern point of the Virginian peninsula, and has remained in the hands of the Federal Government since the outbreak of the war. This fortress, crossing its fire with that of the Rip Raps, a fort built on an artificial island, commands the passage from the Atlantic to Hampton Roads, and thence by the James river to Richmond, or by the Elizabeth to Norfolk, where the Merrimac was then lying. It was in these interior waters that the naval battles had occurred which have filled such a place in public attention, and which exercised upon the future of the Army of the Potomac so serious an influence, that it will not perhaps be improper to give them a place in this narrative.

I shall not describe the Merrimac, which everybody now knows. I will simply remind the reader that she was an old and very large screw steam frigate, razeed to the water line, and covered with an iron roof, inclined just far enough to throw off any ball which might strike her. In this roof portholes were made for 100-pounder Armstrong guns, and for other pieces of very heavy calibre. The bows were armed with an iron spur, resembling that of the ancient galleys. On the 8th of March, the Merrimac, escorted by several iron-clad gunboats, leaves the Elizabeth river and steers straight for the mouth of the James, where lay anchored the two old-fashioned sailing frigates, the Cumberland and Congress. Both open with full broadsides upon the unexpected enemy, but without effect; the balls ricochet from the iron roof. The Merrimac keeps quietly on, and at a speed of no more than from four to five knots strikes her spur into the side of the Cumberland. It is a singular fact that the shock was so slight as to be scarcely perceptible on board the Merrimac; but it had smitten the federal frigate to death. She was seen to careen and go down majestically, carrying with her two hundred men of her crew, who, to the last moment, worked their useless guns;

a grand and glorious spectacle! But in this fatal shock the Merrimac had broken her spur. Was this her reason for not even attempting to sink the Congress? It is at least certain that she confined herself to an artillery duel with the latter frigate. Encumbered with the dead and the dying the Congress set her sails, ran ashore, hauled down her flag, and burst into flames. In attempting to capture part of her crew, the sailors of the Merrimac were exposed to a musketry fire from the shore, and a ball struck her brave and skillful commander, Captain Buchanan.

Meanwhile, the federal squadron united in Hampton Roads, got under weigh to come to the help of their unfortunate companions in the James river: but this squadron could afford them but little help. It was composed of three frigates, of which one alone, the Minnesota, was in a condition to be of any service; this vessel was a screw frigate of the size of the Merrimac, but she was not iron-clad. The two others, the Roanoke, a screw frigate which had lost her mainmast and the St. Lawrence, an old sailing frigate, were only good to be destroyed. Both of these vessels, after fruitless efforts to reach the scene of action, and after partially running aground, gave up the attempt and returned to their anchorage. As to the Minnesota, which might have had some chance against the Merrimac, not with her guns, but by using her superior speed to run her aboard and sink her by the shock, she drew six feet of water more than the Merrimac, and obeyed her helm very badly when she had no more than one foot of water under her keel, and so she, too, ran aground in a very dangerous situation. There is no doubt that if the Merrimac had attacked her here she would have shared the fate of the Cumberland and the Congress. The Merrimac, probably to avenge her captain, remained off the camp of Newport News, shelling that and the batteries, and then returned to Norfolk, where she went in for the night, probably intending to come out the next day and finish her work of destruction. But during the night the Monitor arrived.

I must ask to be pardoned for the familiar comparison which I am about to use to give the reader an idea of this singular vessel.

Everybody knows the cylindrical Savoy biscuits covered with chocolate paste, which are a principal ornament of every pastry cook's shop. Let the reader imagine one of these biscuits placed in an oblong plate, and he will have an exact idea of the external appearance of the Monitor. The Savoy biscuit stands for an iron tower pierced with two openings through which peer the muzzles of two enormous cannons. This tower is made to turn upon its axis by a very ingenious contrivance, in such a fashion as to direct its fire on any point of the horizon. As to the oblong plate on which the biscuit reposes, this is a kind of lid of iron set on at the water level upon the hull which contains the engine, the storage for provisions, and for the crew, and the displacement of the hull supports the whole structure. From a distance the tower only is visible, and this floating tower, so novel in appearance, was the first thing which greeted the Merrimac and her comrades when, on the morning of the 9th of March, they came back to give the final blow to the Minnesota, which was still ashore, and probably to work further ruin.

The two hostile ships, Jamestown and Yorktown, advanced first, with that sort of timid curiosity which a dog displays when he comes near an unknown animal. They had not long to wait, two flashes sprang from the tower, and were followed by the hissing of two 120-pound balls. No more was needed to send the two scouts flying back. The Merrimac, also, at once perceived that there was work ahead, and ran boldly down to meet this unexpected adversary. Then began the duel which has been so much discussed, and which seems destined to bring on so great a revolution in the naval art. From the first, the two tilters felt that they must fight at close quarters; but, even at a few yards distance, they seemed to be equally invulnerable. The balls ricochetted and struck without appearing to leave any trace but the very slightest bruises. Round shot of 120 pounds, conical 100-pounders, Armstrong balls, nothing went through. Then the Merrimac, trying to take advantage of her huge mass, undertook to sink her enemy by taking her violently in flank. But she could not get sufficient way. The Monitor, short, agile, easily handled, ran up to her, ran around her, escaped her blows with a speed which the Merrimac, from her excessive length, could not attain. *Nothing could be more curious* than to see the two adversaries turning one about the other, the little Monitor describing the inner circle, both equally watchful for the weak point of the enemy against which to discharge at point blank one of their enormous projectiles. "It was for all the world," said an eye-witness, "like the fight of Heenan with Sayers." So the conflict went on with no visible results for several hours. Once, only, the Merrimac succeeded in striking the side of the Monitor with her bows; but the Monitor wheeled around under the shock like a floating shell, and a very slight indenture left upon her plating was the only damage caused by this tremendous concussion. The exhaustion of the combatants put an end to this struggle. The confederates returned to Norfolk, leaving the Monitor in possession of the field of battle. The Minnesota and the whole flotilla in Hampton Roads were saved, the pigmy had held his own against the giant. It remained to be seen if the latter would make another effort when the stakes should be more tempting, when, instead of seeking to destroy one or two ships of war, there should be a chance of preventing the disembarkation of a whole army of invasion.

These were the circumstances in which I arrived at Fortress Monroe. Soon the Roads were filled with vessels coming from Alexandria or Annapolis, and filled, some with soldiers, some with horses, cannon and munitions of all kinds. Sometimes I counted several hundred vessels at the anchorage, and among them twenty or twenty-five large steam transports waiting for their turn to come up to the quay and land the fifteen or twenty thousand men whom they brought. The reader may judge how fearful would have been the catastrophe had the Merrimac suddenly appeared among this swarm of ships, striking them one after another and sending to the bottom these human hives with all their inmates! The federal authorities both naval and military here underwent several days of the keenest anxiety. Every time that a smoke was seen above the trees which concealed the Elizabeth river, men's hearts beat fast; but the Merrimac never came; she allowed the landing to take place without opposition.

Why did she do this?

She did not come because her position at Norfolk as a constant menace secured without any risk two results of great importance. In the first place she kept paralysed in Hampton Roads the naval forces assembled to join the land army in the attack upon Yorktown: in the second place, and this was her principal object, she deprived the federal army of all the advantages which the possession of the James would have secured to it in a campaign of which Richmond was the base.

No doubt, if the Merrimac had gone down to the Roads and destroyed the fleet there assembled, she would have achieved an immense result, but all the chances would not have been with her in such an enterprise. In the first place, the Merrimac would have encountered the Monitor. Ship to ship she did not fear this enemy: the Monitor's armament had proved impotent against her armor and would prove so again; and if she had not succeeded in sinking the Monitor at the first shock she had taken her measures to secure better luck the next time.

The expedient adopted was a submarine spur of hammered steel, ten feet long with which she would have reached the hull of the Monitor below her iron cover. Of course the latter floating at the water level and without compartments must have gone down as soon as she fairly made water. But the Monitor would have had new auxiliaries in a new conflict When the Merrimac first came out, as she was seen to make nothing of piercing the Cumberland and sinking that unlucky ship, it had instantly occurred to the federals that in the ab sence of vessels constructed like herself the best means of fight ing her would be to employ large vessels of great speed, which might be brought together to the number of five or six and driven against her as soon as she should make her appearance. The engines of these ships once set in motion, only five or six men would be required to guide them. The men and the ships were ready. Had the Merrimac appeared they would have run down upon her at twice her speed. One at least must have succeeded in striking her broadside and would have infallibly sunk her, for her cuirass offered no defence against such an attack, or must have run her aboard at the stern and deranged her screw when the Monitor would have had her at her mercy. Other precautions had been taken. A net-work of submarine cordage had been set at the mouth of the Elizabeth river, and this would probably not have failed to sweep around the Merrimac's screw and paralyse its working. All these things, but especially the five or six large vessels with steam always up, and always on the watch like a pack of dogs straining at the leash, had brought the confederate authorities to reflection. For my own part, I am perfectly satisfied that if the Merrimac had ventured into the deep water, beyond the shoals which obstruct the entrance of the James and Elizabeth, where her adversaries could get way upon them, she would have gone down in a few moments. The federal officers appreciating the importance of the object aimed at were deter mined to sacrifice their ships and with their ships their own lives to attain it.

In a word, the American navy might prevent the Merrimac from coming into deep water and interfering with the military operations, of which the York river was the destined theatre. But the Merrimac, on the other hand, stood in the way of similar operations on the James. This was an immense service to be rendered by a single ship! We have seen above how impossible it became to move forward the army of the Potomac directly and by land upon Richmond, when the railway lines, by which it was to be supplied and its different parts united, were interrupted. Here we see the direct road to Richmond by water blocked by a vessel, a wreck happily rescued from the destruction of the Norfolk navy yard, fished up half burned from the bottom of a dock, and transformed by hands as intelligent as they were daring, into a formidable warlike machine. Instead of moving up the bank of the James river to Richmond rapidly under the escort and with the support of a powerful flotilla, here was the whole federal army compelled to disembark under great perils at Fortress Monroe in order to take the practicable but long and round-about road of the York river. We were to be forced into going first to Yorktown, an obstacle to be removed by arms, and then into ascending the York and the Pamunkey to the head waters at White House. From this point where we must leave our gunboats, we were then to follow the line of the York river railway, a road on which there were happily no bridges, and which it was not therefore easy to cut, but which traverses an unwholesome region, and offers the formidable barrier of the Chickahominy river at a few miles from Richmond.

A sure and rapid operation was thus converted into a long and hazardous campaign, simply because we had lost on one point, and for a short time, the control of the water. Every body had doubted the efficiency of iron-clads, and nobody had thought much of the Merrimac before we learned what she was. This skepticism was cruelly punished. In the West the armies of the Union were going on from success to success, thanks to the coöperation, energy, and enterprise of the navy, admirably seconded by the geographical formation of the country. Here things were very different. A single success of the confederates by sea, a single blow which they had succeeded in striking by surprise, was destined perhaps to paralyze the whole federal army, to make it lose great geographical advantages equal to those which existed in the West, and to compromise, or at least to postpone the success of its operations; so true is it that experience has not yet taught even the most experienced maritime nations all that is to be gained by the coöperation of a well-organized navy in wars by land!

III.

From Fortress Monroe to Williamsburg.

Whilst we were thus waiting and waiting in vain for the Merrimac, the army was landing at Fortress Monroe, now the scene of a prodigious activity. By the 4th of April, six divisions, the cavalry, the reserve, and an immense number of wagons had been landed. The General-in-Chief who had arrived the evening before, put them at once in motion. Keyes, with three divisions took the road which leads along the banks of the James river. McClellan with the rest of the army followed the direct road to Yorktown. We came at once upon the ruins of Hampton, burned down some months before, *a la Rostopchin*, by the confederate General Magruder. We were informed that he still commanded the garrison of Yorktown and the Peninsula. Magruder, like all the confederate leaders, had belonged to the regular army of the Union down to the moment of the insurrection. His former comrades, now at the head of the federal troops, were familiar with his habits and character, and sought to infer from them the course he would pursue. This reciprocal knowledge which the chiefs of the two armies possessed of each other, the result of a career begun in common in early youth at the military school, and pursued either on the battle-field or in the tedious life of frontier garrisons, was certainly a singular trait of this singular war. Some people built up their hopes of a final reconciliation upon these old intimacies, but such hopes were not to be realized.

Another not less curious trait of the war, which appeared in the outset of the campaign and was constantly reproduced, was the complete absence of all information in regard to the country and to the position of the enemy, the total ignorance under which we labored in regard to his movements, and the number of his troops. The few inhabitants we met were hostile and dumb; the deserters and negroes generally told us much more than they knew in order to secure a welcome, and as we had no maps and no knowledge of localities, it was impossible to make anything of their stories, and to reconcile their often contradictory statements.

We were here twenty-four miles from Yorktown, and we could not learn what works the enemy had thrown up, nor what was his force within them. This was the more amazing that Fortress Monroe had always been held by a strong garrison, which ought to have been able to obtain some information or to make some reconnoissance in this direction. But by a strange aberration, this fortress now become the base of operations of the Army of the Potomac, had been specially sequestered from the command of General McClellan, together with its garrison, although the General in charge of it was his inferior in rank. Hence arose military susceptibilities which were by no means favorable to the exchange of confidential communications.

So the Army of the Potomac moved on in the dark toward Yorktown. We were two days on the road. The column of the General-in-Chief had passed some fortified positions abandoned by the enemy. A few horsemen were occasionally seen at rare intervals. No sooner had we come under the walls of Yorktown than we were arrested by the cannon. A few gunboats, which had appeared at the mouth of York river, had found it guarded by some forty pieces of heavy calibre. The naval officers concluded that they could not pass this battery; the investment of the place by water must consequently be abandoned. When we undertook to invest it by land, we came upon a series of works stretching across the peninsula, on the edge of a marshy stream, called Warwick Creek, and high enough to make investment impossible. The confederates had dammed this marshy stream in places so as to convert it into a pond, and their dams, with other accessible points, were defended by artillery, redoubts, and rifle-pits. Abattis had been formed in front of these redoubts and upon the opposite side of the marsh so as to secure a wide range for the guns.

General Keyes, in trying to pass the river Warwick, had been the first to encounter this line of defence. His march had been very slow. The country, perfectly flat, and covered with marshy forests, was only traversed by a few roads scarce worthy of the name. The rain, falling in torrents, unusual at this season of the year, had made these roads, if we must so call them, completely impracticable. The infantry could contrive to get on by marching in the water through the woods, but as soon as two or three wagons had made ruts in the ground, no wheeled vehicle could move an inch. Of course all movement was impossible, for we could not leave the wagons. The country was utterly deserted. Except water and food, it supplied us with nothing. The soldiers, unaccustomed either to long marches or to carry their ammunition, carried but two days' provisions. These exhausted, the wagons were their only resource. Then it was that we had to make what in America are called corduroy roads. These are made by cutting down trees of the same size, a few inches in diameter, and laying them side by side on the ground. All the infantry, not on duty at the advanced posts, were employed, working up to their knees in the mud and water, upon this Herculean labor, and they got through it wonderfully. Here the American pioneer was in his element; the roads were made as if by enchantment. The cannon and the wagons came in slowly indeed, but they came in where it seemed an impossibility they ever should do so. At night the troops could find no dry corner for their bivouac. They had to sit down on the trunks of felled trees, or to construct with logs a sort of platform, on which they snatched a very precarious rest. I remember to have seen a general of division whose whole establishment consisted of five or six pine branches, one end stuck in the mud, or rather in the water, the other resting on a tree. Here he slept with an indian-rubber cloak over his head. Marching along in this fashion, we reached the confederate lines, which opened on us at once with a sharp fire of artillery. We replied, but without making any impression on the well-defined works which covered the hostile cannon. The creek had been reconnoitred and found impassable by infantry, both on account of the depth of water and of its marshy borders, in which the troops would have been mired under a cross-fire of numbers of sharpshooters, concealed in the woods and behind the embankments.

Throughout the seven miles of the confederate lines we encountered the same attitude of alert defence. Everywhere cannon and camps. Of course the inference was that we were arrested by forces apparently formidable and before a position not easily to be carried. But this case had been foreseen. In order to gain time, and avoid the tedium of a siege, General McClellan had thought out the means of turning the position. The enemy held the James, with the Merrimac and his gun boats; the York was closed by the Yorktown and Gloucester Point batteries. Nevertheless, by a disembarkation on the Severn, beyond Gloucester, we might carry the latter position and open the way of the federal gunboats into the river York. A subsequent movement up the left bank, in the direction of West Point, would put us so far in the rear of the army charged with the defence of the lines of Yorktown, that it would have been in a most perilous position. This accomplished, the confederates must have abandoned Gloucester, and fallen back hastily upon Richmond. The execution of this *coup de main* had been left to a corps of the army commanded by General McDowell. This corps was to be the last to embark at Washington, and it was calculated that it ought to reach Yorktown in a body on its transports at the moment when the rest of the army, moving by land, should appear before that post from Fortress Monroe.

Instead of finding it, we received the inexplicable and as yet unexplained intelligence that this *corps*, 35,000 strong, had been sent to another destination. The news was received in the army with stupefaction, although the majority could not foresee the deplorable consequences of a step taken, it must be supposed, with no evil intention, but certainly with inconceivable recklessness. Fifteen days before, this measure, although it must always have been injurious, would have been much less so. We might have made arrangements upon a new basis. Taken when it was it deranged a whole system of machinery fairly at work. Among the divisions of McDowell's corps, there was one, that of Franklin, which was more regretted than all the others, as well on account of the troops themselves, as of their commanders. The General-in-Chief had bestowed special pains on its organization during the winter, and earnestly demanded its restoration. It was sent back to him without a word of explanation, precisely as it had been detached from him. This fine division, 11,000 strong, arrived, and for a moment the General thought of intrusting to it alone the Gloucester expedition. But this intention was renounced.

Then came the reflection, that somewhere in these seven miles of confederate intrenchments, there must be a weak spot.

Could this spot be found and forced, the usual result in such cases would probably come to pass. The enemy at either extremity would suppose themselves to have been turned, and would become demoralized. If we then continued to pour a constantly increasing force of our troops through the opening thus made, we would probably inflict upon the army thus cut in two one of those disasters which settle the fate of a campaign.

This weak point, it was supposed, had been found near the centre of the lines of Warwick Creek, at a place called Lee's Mill. The bottom here was firm, the water waist deep. In front of the hostile works was a kind of open plateau, upon which a strong artillery force might be brought up to shatter them. On the 16th of April, an attempt was made at this point. Eighteen field-pieces opened fire at 500 yards on the confederate batteries, and silenced them, and the creek was then passed by some Vermont companies.

They advanced gallantly, carried a rifle-pit, but their ammunition had been wetted in passing the stream; they were not supported, and retired after losing many of their number. The project thus began was, no doubt, found to present unforeseen difficulties, and it was at once abandoned.

This operation, like that against Gloucester, not being feasible, we were forced to undertake the siege of the uninvested fortifications of Yorktown.

The various attempts at feeling our way had unfortunately consumed much time, and the siege itself was to consume much more, although it was pushed forward with great energy. Ten thousand laborers, constantly relieved, were set at work on the abattis, through the woods, roads, trenches and batteries. It was a curious spectacle. A narrow arm of the sea, fringed by a close and vigorous vegetable growth, made up of trees of all kinds, living and dead, draped in vines and mosses, wound up towards the front of our attack. This had been used as our first parallel. Bridges were thrown over it, roads had been opened on the banks among the tulip trees, the Judas trees, and the azaleas in full flower. From this natural parallel others set out, made by human hands and rapidly approaching the works. The defenders kept up on all that they saw or suspected, a tremendous fire. The shells whistled from every side among the high trees, tore off the branches, scared the horses, but did very little damage. Nobody heeded them. In the evenings when all the squads came in in good order, their guns on their backs and their picks on their shoulders, the firing increased, as if the enemy had marked the hour. We used to go to the front for this cannonade, as if it were an entertainment, and when on fine spring evenings the troops came in gaily to the sound of martial music through the blossoming woods, and when the balloon which we used for our reconnoissances was floating in the air, one easily believed himself to be enjoying a festival, and was glad for a moment to forget the miseries of the war.

All this time the siege went on. A powerful artillery force had been brought up, not without difficulty. Rifled guns of 100 and even of 200 pounds calibre, 13-inch mortars, were got ready to batter the works. Fourteen batteries had been built, armed and provisioned. If we had not yet opened a fire it was because we meant it to be general from all sides, and we were only waiting to get into a complete state of preparation. It was impossible, however, to resist the desire we had of trying our 200-pounders. These enormous guns were worked with inconceivable ease. Four men were able to load and point them with no more trouble than our old-fashioned 24-pounders. At three miles their fire was admirably accurate. One day one of these huge guns had a sort of duel with a somewhat smaller rifled piece mounted on one of the bastions of Yorktown. The curious upon our side got upon the parapets to watch the effect of every shot, then whilst we were discussing our observations the sentinel would warn us that the enemy in his turn was firing; but the distance was so great that between the discharge and the arrival of the ball everybody had time enough to step quietly down and get under the shelter of the parapet. Nevertheless, such was the excellence of the firing that you were sure to see the enormous missile pass over the very place where the group of spec tators had a moment before been standing. It would then go on and strike the ground 50 yards in the rear, its cap would explode and it would burst, throwing into the air a cloud of earth as high as the jet of the water-works at St. Cloud.

These new and curious artillery experiences were not the only interesting feature of this siege. In 1781 Yorktown had been besieged by the combined forces of France and America under Washington and Rochambeau, and this operation had resulted in the celebrated capitulation which secured the independence of the United States. At every step we came upon the traces of this first siege. Here in this decrepid hovel Lafayette had fixed his head-quarters; there the French trenches began; there, again, lay the camp of the regiments of Bourbon and of Saintonge. In other directions appeared the still visible entrenchments of Rochambeau, upon which the almost tropical vegetation of the country had reasserted it empire. Further on was pointed out to us the house inhabited by the two commanders. Behind these same fortifications of Yorktown, Cornwallis and his Englishmen had so long withstood the assault of the allied armies. Upon yonder ramparts the blood of our soldiers had sealed an alliance unbroken down to our own times; an alliance to which the United States once owed their prosperity and their greatness. Not to speak of the emotion with which I found myself in this distant spot surrounded by recollections of national glory; not to speak of the interest with which I examined the traces of scenes of war, some of the actors in which I had myself been permitted to see, I could not but ask myself if by a strange caprice of destiny these same ramparts might not behold the undoing of the work of 1781, and if from the slow siege of Yorktown, both the ruin of the great Republic and the rupture of the Franco-American alliance might not be fated to come forth. The destiny of the Union was in the hand of the God of Battles. No one could foresee his decrees; but the Franco-American alliance, that alliance which had so well served all generous ideas, was more plainly dependent upon human will. Doubtless the strife before Yorktown was a civil war, and although the federals were fighting for the most just of all possible causes, nothing absolutely obliged France to send her soldiers to aid them. But the sword of France makes itself felt afar as well as nearer home, and the Americans of the North could have wished to see their ancient allies throw their influence in favor of the side on which were arrayed justice and liberty.

It was plain that with the powerful means which we were using the fall of Yorktown was purely a question of time. Crushed under the weight of the fire about to be opened upon them, without casemates to shelter their troops, with no other defences than earthworks and palisades, the rebels had no chance of prolonged resistance. Everything was ready for the decisive blow. Not only was a terrible bombardment to be directed against the city: not only were the choicest troops selected for the grand assault which was to follow the bombardment, but the steam transports waited only for the signal to pass up into the York river as soon as the place should fall, and land the forces of Franklin high up on the line of the confederate retreat. A part of the forces were actually kept on board of the transports. In a few hours they would have passed over the distance which it would have taken the enemy two days to traverse. Driven by storm from Yorktown, followed up step for step, intercepted on their road by fresh troops, the army of the South would have been in a very critical position, and the Federals would have found what they so greatly needed, a brilliant military success.

This they needed, not only to escape the serious evils with which they were threatened by a prolongation of the campaign; the political was perhaps more urgent than the military necessity. A victory and a decisive victory alone, could bring on the re-establishment of the Union, that object of the ardent pursuit of all American patriots who set the greatness and the prosperity of their country above the passions of parties and of sects. Bull Run, by humbling one of the adversaries, had for a time shut the door upon all hopes of reconciliation. As soon as the legal government of the country should have recovered its ground, and proved its strength, it would again become possible to negotiate and to establish, by a common agreement, the fraternal bonds of the Union. To secure this, it was necessary to lose no time. The minds of men were embittering on either side; interests, individual ambitions, foreign intrigues were daily exerting a more active interposition between the two camps, and every delay must make the work of reconciliation more difficult. A great success of the federal army before Yorktown was then of vital importance to the Government at Washington. Unfortunately, the confederate leaders and generals saw and felt this also; and like skillful men they took the best way of preventing it.

In the night of the 3d and 4th of May, Yorktown and the lines of Warwick river were evacuated. This evacuation must have been commenced several days before, but it had been managed with great secresy and great skill. On the 3d, the fire of the hostile batteries had greatly increased in intensity. The shells from the rifled guns flew in all directions with a length of range which had not before been suspected. The accuracy of their fire* forced us to abandon all the signal posts we had established in the tops of the tallest trees. The balloon itself, whenever it rose in the air, was saluted with an iron hail of missiles which were, however, perfectly harmless. The object of all this was to mask the retreat, and it was perfectly successful.

On the 4th, at daybreak, the men in the rifle-pits of the advance saw no signs of the foe before them. A few of them ventured cautiously up to the very lines of the enemy. All was as silent as death. Soon suspicion grew into certainty; it was flashed upon the head-quarters by all the telegraphic lines which connected them with the different corps of the army. The confederates had vanished, and with them all chances of a brilliant victory. The impossibility of any naval coöperation, and the fatal measures by which the Army of the Potomac lost the corps of McDowell, had combined with the firmness of the enemy to prevent us from taking Yorktown by storm. We had next spent a whole month in constructing gigantic works now become useless, and now, after all this, the confederates fell back, satisfied with gaining time to prepare for the defence of Richmond, and henceforth relying on the season of heats and sickness for aid against the federal army encamped among the marshes of

* Note.—I am not sure whether I ought to attribute to this accuracy an extraordinary fact which occurred during the siege. Some topographical engineers were busy estimating a relief. They were perceived, and a single shot was fired at them. The shell, fired from an immense distance, burst upon the circumferentor and killed the officer and his assistant.

Virginia. The federals, whose number was constantly lessening, saw before them the perspective of a campaign which threatened to become more and more laborious, diminishing daily as its perils increased the chances of an amicable adjustment. Here was matter enough for serious and even for melancholy reflection: but in war moments are precious, and it is weakness to lose them in lamentations. It was probable that the enemy was at no great distance. He could not yet have gained any considerable start, and by throwing ourselves rapidly upon his track we might at least come up with his rear guard, fling it into disorder, and make some prisoners.

A few hours after the news was received of the evacuation, the whole army was in motion. Stoneman's cavalry first crossed the intrenchments. As they passed on, several infernal machines, cowardly instruments of destruction, burst under the horses' feet and killed several men.

We had only time to cast a single glance upon the formidable works thrown up by the enemy, upon which he had abandoned 72 pieces of artillery; then passing swiftly through his deserted camps and burning magazines, amid which the sound of sudden explosions was heard from time to time, we took the road to Williamsburg, a small city situated upon a point at which the Virginian peninsula, shut closely in between two arms of the sea, offers a strong and defensible position. It was upon this isthmus that we expected to come up with the rear guard of the enemy.

Stoneman marched rapidly upon Williamsburg with all the cavalry and four batteries of horse artillery. The infantry followed as fast as the few and narrow roads would permit. There were really only two of these roads—one direct from Yorktown, the other coming from the left of the federal positions. The latter traversed Warwick river at Lee's Mill, on a bridge which it took three hours to rebuild. When Smith's division, which was the first to cross, had advanced a short distance it met a portion of the confederate army, which gave way and fell back before it. Smith informed McClellan of this, and the General, who thought that Stoneman might outstrip the hostile column and cut it off at the fork of the roads before Williamsburg, sent orders to that officer to hasten his march. Unfortunately, it was not easy to advance rapidly. The roads, and particularly that road taken by the cavalry, were narrow and full of frightful morasses from which it was difficult to extricate the cannon, although the weather had been fine and dry for several days. At any other time we should have paused to admire the scenery of this lovely region covered with virgin forests broken at intervals by a clearing, and recalling by its aspect the smiling districts of Devonshire, that Provence of England. But now we only looked upon these forests as the hiding places of an enemy. The young Duke of Chartres, on a scout with forty horsemen, suddenly fell upon a confederate brigade. This was the rear guard of the column described by Smith. The prince brought back some fifteen prisoners and gave his information to Stoneman, who hurried his advance to reach this column before it should join the body of the hostile forces supposed to be at Williamsburg. Soon the fork of the two roads was reached, the one leading from Yorktown, by which Stoneman was advancing, and the other leading from Lee's Mill, by which the confederates were retreating. But the moment that the federal cavalry came out upon this fork, it was received by an artillery fire from numerous field works erected in front of Williamsburg. A rapid survey explained the position. As we have stated, the Virginian peninsula narrows towards Williamsburg. Two creeks or bays, the one opening out of the James, the other out of the York, and both terminating in marshes, make this neck of land still smaller, and form between the marshes a kind of isthmus upon which the roads from Lee's Mill and from Yorktown debouch. To the south

4

of the isthmus, that is to say in the direction of the approach from Yorktown, the country is densely wooded. To the north, on the contrary, that is to say towards Williamsburg, it is open and exhibits large fields of grain behind which the spires and towers of the city are visible. Upon this open space, the enemy had erected first, a considerable bastioned work, Fort Magruder, placed upon the roadway opposite the. isthmus, and then a series of redoubts and rifle-pits fronting every part of the marsh over which it would have been possible for infantry to advance. He had then constructed vast abattis in such wise as to expose to his artillery and musketry the approaches of the marsh and of the fork of the roads. It was in the midst of these abattis that the federal cavalry debouched upon the trot; and here it was, that they were saluted with a shower of shells from Fort Magruder. In the space between this fort and the redoubts, the confederate foot and horse were drawn up in order of battle. Stoneman, seeing that the enemy covered the fork of the roads, and perceiving that it would be impossible for him to maintain his ground before them, undertook to dislodge them by a vigorous blow. He threw forward all his horse artillery, which took up its positions brilliantly in front of the abattis, and replied to the fire of the redoubts; and he then ordered his cavalry to charge. The sixth federal cavalry dashed forward gallantly to meet the cavalry of the confederates, passed directly under the cross-fire of the redoubts, and rode into one of those fights with the cold steel which have become so rare in these days. Nevertheless, this was all so much valor thrown away. The enemy did not disturb himself; he had the advantages of number and position. To carry these works with cavalry was impossible. Men and particularly horses, began to fall. "I have lost thirty-one men," said Major Williams, who had led the charge of the sixth, gracefully saluting General Stoneman with his sabre, with that air of determination which says, "we will go at it again, but it's of no use."

Stoneman then ordered the retreat. We repassed the abattis, and falling back to a clearing about half a mile distant, there awaited the arrival of the infantry to renew the engagement. Unluckily, in traversing the marsh, a gun of the horse-artillery got buried in the mud and could not be extricated. In vain were the teams doubled. The enemy concentrated his fire of shells on that point and killed all the horses. The gun had to be left. It was the first which the army had lost, and the men were inconsolable. In the evening we renewed our efforts to recover it, but the abattis were filled with hostile sharpshooters who made it impossible to approach. The sun was going down. The confederate columns coming from Lee's Mill, escaped and took shelter behind the entrenchments of Williamsburg. As to the federal infantry, it came up very late. The roads over which it passed had been tremendously obstructed. At nightfall General Sumner, who had assumed command, wished to make an attempt to carry the works. Unfortunately it was completely dark before the troops debouched from the woods and the marshes, and everything had to be put off to the next day. Upon this supervened one of those vexatious mishaps which are too common in war, and of which this army did not escape its full share during this trying campaign. The rain began to fall in torrents and poured down incessantly for thirty consecutive hours. The country became one vast lake, the roads were channels of liquid mud. The troops dismally bivouacked for the night where they stood.

Next day the battle began again, but, of course, in circumstances unfavorable to the federals. The two roads leading to Williamsburg were crowded with troops. Upon that to the left from Lee's Mill, were the divisions of Hooker and Kearney belonging to Heintzelman's corps—but they were separated from each other by an enormous multitude of wagons loaded down with baggage, and for the most part, fast in the mud. Upon that to the right two other divisions were moving forward with still greater difficulty. Such was the condition of the ground that the cannon sank over the axle into the mud. This medley of men and baggage thrown pellmell into narrow and flooded roads had fallen into considerable disorder. In the United States there is no such thing as a corps of the General Staff. The American system of "every man for himself," individually applied by the officers and soldiers of each corps to one another, is also applied by the corps themselves to their reciprocal relations. There is no special branch of the service whose duty it is to regulate, centralize and direct the movements of the army. In such a case as this of which we are speaking, we should have seen the General Staff Officers of a French army taking care that nothing should impede the advance of the troops, stopping a file of wagons here and ordering it out of the road to clear the way, sending on a detail of men there to repair the roadway or to draw a cannon out of the mire, in order to communicate to every corps commander the orders of the General-in-Chief.

Here nothing of the sort is done. The functions of the adjutant-general are limited to the transmission of the orders of the general. He has nothing to do with seeing that they are executed. The general has no one to bear his orders but aides-de-camp who have the best intentions in the world, and are excellent at repeating mechanically a verbal order, but to whom nobody pays much attention if they undertake to exercise any initiative whatever. Down to the present moment although this want of a General Staff had been often felt, its consequences had not been serious. We had the telegraph, which followed the army everywhere and kept up communications between the different corps; the generals could converse together and inform each other of anything that it was important to know. But once on the march this resource was lost to us, and so farewell to our communications!

The want of a General Staff was not less severely felt in obtaining and transmitting the information necessary at the moment of an impending action. No one knew the country; the maps were so defective that they were useless. Little was known about the fortified battle-field on which the army was about to be engaged. Yet this battle-field had been seen and reconnoitred the day before by the troops which had taken part in Stoneman's skirmish. Enough was surely known of it for us to combine a plan of attack and assign to every commander his own part in the work. No, this was not so. Every one kept his observations to himself, not from illwill, but because it was nobody's special duty to do this general work. It was a defect in the organization, and with the best elements in the world an army which is not organized cannot expect great success. It is fortunate if it escape great disaster.

Thanks to this constitutional defect of the federal armies, Hooker's division which led the column on the left hand road and had received, the day before, a general order to march upon Williamsburg, came out on the morning of the 5th upon the scene of Stoneman's cavalry fight without the least knowledge of what it was to meet there. Received as soon as it appeared with a steady fire from the hostile works, it deployed resolutely in the abattis and went into action. But it came up little by little and alone, whilst the defence was carried on by from 15 to 20,000 men strongly entrenched. The odds were too great.

Hooker, who is an admirable soldier, held his own for some time, but he had to give way and fall back, leaving in the woods and in these terrible abattis some two thousand of his men killed and wounded, with several of his guns which he could not bring off. The enemy followed him as he fell back. The division of General Kearney having passed the crowded road, and marching upon the guns at the *pas de course*, re-established the battle. The fight had now rolled from the edges of the plain into the forest, and it was sharp, for the enemy was strongly reinforced. The federals fought not less firmly, encouraged by their chiefs, Hooker, Heintzelman, and Kearney. Kearney in especial, who lost an arm in Mexico, and fought with the French at the Muzaia and at Solferino, had displayed the finest courage. All his aids had fallen around him, and left alone he had electrified his men by his intrepidity. During all this time the part of the army massed on the road to the right remained passive. A single division only had come up, and the generals in command could not resolve to throw it into the engagement without seeing its supports. These supports were delayed by the swollen streams, the encumbered roads, the shattered wagons sticking in the mud.

But all the while the sound of Hooker's musketry was in our ears. His division was cut up and falling back. His guns had been heard at first in front, then on one side, and they were receding still. The balls and the shells began to whistle and shatter the trees over the fresh division as it stood immovable and expectant.

It was now three o'clock, and the generals resolved to act. One division passed through the woods to flank the regiments which were driving Hooker, while to the extreme right a brigade passed the creek on an old mill bridge, which the enemy had failed to secure, and debouched upon the flank of the Williamsburg works. The confederates did not expect this attack, which, if successful, must sweep everything before it. They dispatched two brigades, which advanced resolutely through the corn fields to drive back the federals. The latter coolly allowed their foes to come up, and received them with a tremendous fire of artillery. The confederates unshaken, pushed on within thirty yards of the cannon's mouth, shouting, "Bull Run! Bull Run!" as the Swiss used to shout, "Granson! Granson!" There, however, they wavered, and the federal General Hancock, seizing the moment, cried to his soldiers, as he waved his cap, "Now, gentlemen, the bayonet!" and charged with his brigade. The enemy could not withstand the shock, broke and fled, strewing the field with his dead. At this very moment General McClellan, who had been detained at Yorktown, appeared on the field. It was dusk, the night was coming on, the rain still falling in torrents. On three sides of the plateau on which the general was, the cannon and the musketry were rattling uninterruptedly. The success of Hancock had been decisive, and the reserves brought up by the General-in-Chief, charging upon the field settled the affair. Then it was that I saw General McClellan, passing in front of the Sixth cavalry, give his hand to Major Williams with a few words on his brilliant charge of the day before. The regiment did not hear what he said, but it knew what he meant, and from every heart went up one of those masculine, terrible shouts, which are only to be heard on the field of battle. These shouts, taken up along the whole line, struck terror to the enemy. We saw them come upon the parapets and look out in silence and motionless upon the scene. Then the firing died away and night fell on the combat which in America is called "the battle of Williamsburg.

IV.

From Williamsburg to Fair Oaks.

THE next day dawned clear and cloudless. The atmosphere had that purity which in warm countries succeeds a storm; the woods breathed all the freshness of a fair spring morning. All around us lay a smiling landscape, decked with splendid flowers new to European eyes; but all this only deepened the mournful contrast of the battle field, strewn with the dead and dying, with wrecks and ruin. The confederates had evacuated their works during the night. We soon entered them and watched the blue lines of the federal infantry as they marched with banners flying into the town of Williamsburg to the sound of expl·ding magazines and caissons. Shortly after the General's staff came in by a broad fine street, bordered with acacias. All the shops were shut, but the inhabitants for the most part were to be seen in their doorways and windows, looking on us with a sombre, anxious air. The negròes alone were smiling. Many of them put on the most grotesquely victorious airs, or decamped in the direction of Fortress Monroe, that is to say, of freedom, carrying their wives and children with them in small carts. From all the public buildings, churches, colleges and the like waved the yellow flag. They were crowded with the wounded left there by the enemy. At the end of a broad street, we debouched upon a handsome square, ornamented with a marble statue of Lord Botetourt, once governor of Virginia, and surrounded by the buildings of a celebrated college founded by the English Government when Virginia was a pet colony. The wounded were lying upon the very steps of the college porticoes.

General McClellan's first thought was for the relief of all this suffering. He dispatched a flag of truce to the confederate rear-guard, to request them to send in surgeons to look after their wounded, promising them perfect freedom of action. A number of these medical officers soon arrived, dressed in the dull-gray confederate uniform with the green collar, which gave them the appearance of Austrian Chasseurs.

This duty done, the next thing was to station sentinels for the maintenance of exact discipline. This precaution was superfluous, for if the obedience of the federal soldiers to their officers is not what it should be, for the good of the service, I venture to believe that no army has ever shown more respect for non-combatants and private property. During the whole time of my presence with the Army of the Potomac, the only instance of disorder which came to my knowledge, was the pillage of a garret filled with the finest Virginia tobacco, which was discovered in an abandoned barn. Let me add that the circumstances made this strict observance of discipline particularly meritorious. The troops encamped around Williamsburg after the battle which we have just described were for a short time in want of provisions in consequence of the impracticable state of the roads, and they endured with resignation the hostile attitude of the inhabitants who met their offers to pay in specie for food with an unanimous refusal. After the first moment of fear had passed, and it was evident that there was no ground for alarm, the ladies of the town might have been seen ostentatiously carrying to the wounded of their own party the refreshments which could not be procured for the wounded federals ; and whenever, followed by their negro servants carrying well filled baskets, they met a federal soldier on the sidewalk, they made a point of gathering up their dresses in haste as if to avoid the contact of some unclean animal. The victors only smiled at these childish and ill-bred demonstrations. Other troops in their place might have been less patient.

The General fixed his head-quarters in the house which the confederate General Johnston had occupied the day before, for it was no longer with Magruder that we were dealing. Johnston is considered by friends and foes, and especially by his old comrades of the regular army, as a warrior of the first rank. He is reputed to unite great personal courage with an iron will, and a remarkable capacity for taking in a whole battle field at a glance. With the fine intellect of Jefferson Davis to conceive, his omnipotence to prepare, and Johnston to execute their plans, the confederates were in good hands, as we very plainly saw. By holding his position for two days before Williamsburg, Johnston had given time for his trains and f : the major part of his troops to move quietly off through the narrow country roads; and notwithstanding the rain which had reduced these roads to a deplorable condition, he reached the upper York river two days after the battle of Williamsburg, in time to engage the troops of Franklin, then just disembarked, and so complete the protection of his retreat. We were next to meet him before Richmond.

The federal army passed three days at Williamsburg looking up the wounded who were scattered through the woods, and burying the dead. The wounded were sent off by water to the North on board of those large steamboats which are so famous for their comfort and their elegance. Thanks to the creeks which cut up the whole country, these boats, came up and took the wounded almost from the battle field. As to the dead they were buried where they lay. On the side of the enemy they were numerous; we counted sixty-three in a single rifle-pit. General McClellan sent a few squadrons in pursuit of the enemy, and these horsemen had several passages at arms with the rear guard. The first day many prisoners were taken and eight cannon; but after the second day the retreat became orderly and the pursuit almost purposeless. Moreover, if the enemy lost some of his guns, he carried off an almost equal number, captured from Hooker's division, which were used as trophies to kindle a zeal already somewhat cooled by his long and continued retreats. The mass of the federal troops was detained by the necessity of waiting for provisions from Yorktown, the arrival of which was retarded by the state of the roads. They came at last, and as the fine weather dried the roads up very fast, a two days' march brought us up with the corps which had disembarked and established a depot at the head of York river. The whole army was collected around this point and then resumed its march to Richmond along the Pamunkey, a navigable affluent of the York. Nothing could be more picturesque than this military march along the banks of a fine stream through a magnificent country arrayed in all the wealth of spring vegetation. The winding course of the Pamunkey through a valley in which meadows of the brightest green alternated with wooded hills, offered a perpetual scene of enchantment to our eyes. Flowers bloomed everywhere, especially on the river banks, which abounded in magnolias, Virginia jessamines, azaleas and blue lupines. Humming-birds, snakes, and strange birds of every hue, sported in the branches and about the trunks of the trees. Occasionally we passed a stately habitation which recalled the old mansions of rural France, with its large windows in the roof; around it a handsome garden, and behind it the slave-cabins.

As the army was descried in the distance, the inhabitants would hang out a white flag. One of the provost marshal's horsemen would dismount at the door, and, reassured by his presence, the ladies in their long muslin dresses, surrounded by a troop of little negresses with frizzled hair and bare legs, would come out upon the verandah and watch the passage of the troops. They were often accompanied by old men, with strongly marked faces, long, white locks, and broad brimmed hats—never by young men. All the men capable of bearing arms had been carried off, willy-nilly, by the Government, to join in the general defence. If an officer dismounted and made his bow to the ladies, he was civilly received. The classic cup of cold water was offered to him in a gourd fixed on the end of a stick, and a melancholy sort of conversation followed. Men and women were eager for the news. They knew nothing of what was happening; the censorship of the confederate newspapers being complete, and the little news they did publish not being often believed. Then the talk turned upon the war. The ladies naturally expressed their hopes for the success of the side on which their brothers were enlisted; but they longed, above all things, for the end of the war and of the incalculable evils it had brought upon the land. "Alas!" we would reply: "who is to blame? Who kindled this unhappy strife? Who fired the first gun without a reason or a motive?" They would make no answer, but their glances would wander mechanically over the black heads crowded in the doors of the negro huts. We never spoke of slavery in these interviews; to utter the word "slave" would have sufficed to call up into the most amiable eyes, an expression of anxiety and of hatred.

At other times we would find the white owners fled, and nobody left but the negroes, with whom we spoke of other matters. I remember a mulatto woman who called our attention with an air of pride to her son, a fine, bright yellow child of some four years, with these significant words: "He is the son of a white man; he is worth 400 dollars. I began at fifteen, and I am nineteen now. I have four already."

So from point to point we moved along the river. The gunboats went first and explored the country before us; then came the topographical officers, moving through the woods with an escort of cavalry, reconnoitering the country, and sketching by the eye and the compass provisional maps, which were photographed at head-quarters for the use of the Generals. The next day, with the help of these maps, the army would get into motion, mingled in masses with its immense team of wagons. About one-fourth of each regiment was occupied in escorting the *materiel* of the corps, piled up, provisions, ammunition, tents and furniture on wagons, at the rate of ten to a battalion. But for the absence of women, we might have been taken for an armed emigration, rather than for soldiers on the march.

The fighting force marched by brigades, followed by their baggage, and these long files of wagons each drawn by four horses or six mules, and driven by a single postilion, made the army stretch upon these narrow forest paths over an immense space of country. Hence followed delays equally immense; for long marches could not have been made without leaving the rear of the columns broken and scattered in the woods by night. Six miles was the extreme limit of our day's march. Sometimes we may have done better; detached corps relieved of all impediments made some long day's marches, but these were exceptions. The troops were in excellent condition. The men were vigorous, strong and intelligent in appearance. The uniform of the whole army was the same; light blue trousers, commonly tucked into the boots, and a blouse or jacket or short tunic of dark blue. Some red mark on the dress distinguished the artillery, a touch of yellow the cavalry. The common head-dress was the *képi*, but many wore a soft black felt hat, with gilded ornaments. The officers, clad like the soldiers, were distinguished by small gilt straps on the shoulder, and a purplish sash. Nothing can be more simple, more comfortable, or more soldier-like than this uniform when it is properly worn. In the evening, when we came to a halt, the camps were formed with much order and regularity. The shelter-tents of the soldiers were put up in the twinkling of an eye. The staffs planted theirs, which were larger and more commodious. The head-quarters was fixed in some central position, with the tent of the General-in-Chief in the middle, and two parallel ranges of tents on either side. The cavalry officers brought in their reports of their reconnoissances and of their constant skirmishes with the enemy. The telegraphers brought on their wires, fastened as usual upon posts, or enveloped in gutta percha and unrolled along the ground from a rapidly driven wagon, which was followed by the operators on horseback with the apparatus slung from their shoulders. All the branches of the service were organized, and the printing office worked as regularly as it could have done at Washington.

Let us do justice to the Americans. They understand this camp-life better than anybody else. Their locomotive habits, the familiarity of many of them with the patriarchal spectacle of emigrant columns moving across the Western prairies, the nomadic life which their officers have led among the Indian tribes, all these things fit them beyond any other soldiers in the world for this kind of life. This encampment of a hundred thousand men, the establishment of this city of tents, was a really curious sight, it recalled the descriptions of the Bible: but there was little that was biblical in the forest of transport ships, most of them steamers, which came up by water under a cloud of smoke as soon as the camp was fixed, and blowing off steam with a loud noise, hauled in to the banks and improvised wharves, which soon became scenes of extraordinary activity. Thousands of wagons hastened in from every side by roads which the axe had opened for them in a few minutes, and returned again loaded with all the commodities required by an army: biscuit, salted meat, coffee, sugar, barley, hay, corn. Then the sick were embarked, and alas! the number of these constantly increased, for the season was at once rainy and intensely hot, and these lovely meadows of the Pamunkey gave birth to deadly fever. Then night would come on disturbed only by the tedious cry of the mocking-bird. With the next morning the flotilla and the army would resume their march, leaving behind them nature silent, but deflowered by their passage.

On May the 16th we reached White House, a fine building once the property of Washington, and now of his descendants, the Lee family. The head of this family, General Lee, was one of the chief officers of the confederate army; one of his nephews was in the federal ranks. General McClellan, always careful to insist upon respect for private property stationed sentinels around the residence of the hostile general, forbade any one to enter it, and would not enter it himself. He planted his tent in a neighboring meadow. This respect for Southern property has been made a reproach to the General in Congress; the opinion of the army did not take this direction; it endorsed the *delicate feeling* of its leader. This feeling was pushed so far that when a general's servants found one day in an abandoned house a basket of champaigne, the General sent it back again conspicuously the next by an aid-de-camp. We may smile at this puritanical austerity to which we are not accustomed in Europe. For my own part I admit that I always admired it.

At White House the Pamunkey ceased to be navigable. The York river railroad, which unites Richmond with this river, crosses it at this point by a bridge which the enemy had destroyed, and then runs in almost a straight line to the Virginian capital. This road had been scarcely injured. Having neither embankments nor viaducts it was not easy to destroy it. A few rails only had been removed, and were soon replaced; all the rolling stock had been run off, but the federal army had locomotives and cars on board of its transports. The whole flotilla was unloaded at White House, where a vast depot was established under the protection of the gunboats, and all the bustle of a seaport soon became visible. The army recommenced its march to Richmond, following the line of the railway, which was to be the vital artery of its operations.

During all this time what were the confederates doing? We have seen Johnston successfully delivering battle against the federal advance, on the 5th of May, at Williamsburg, and against Franklin's corps on the 7th, at the head of York river, in order to gain time for the bulk of his army to fall back undisturbed upon Richmond. Cavalry reconnoissances pushed in all directions had demonstrated the fact that almost the whole hostile army had recrossed the Chickahominy. Everything led us to believe that we should not meet it again excepting under the walls of Richmond; at the same time everything indicated that the confederates were concentrating in their capital for a desperate resistance.

We had captured prisoners belonging to a corps which had, up to this time, been stationed opposite Burnside in North Carolina; it was, therefore, plain that this corps had joined the army of Johnston. We soon learned the evacuation of Norfolk and the occupation of that city by General Wool. It was evident that Davis could only have made up his mind to this sacrifice because he wished to draw into Richmond Huger and the 18,000 men who had up to this time held the great arsenal of Virginia. Finally the confederate leader had ordered a levy *en masse* of all men able to bear arms. They had been sent into camps of instruction, whence they would be incorporated with the old regiments, the effective force of which would thus be doubled. The result of all this threatened the army of the Potomac in its only superiority, that of numbers. Unhappily, too, while the enemy was concentrating and strengthening his forces, ours were melting away. We have already seen how at Alexandria a division was detached and sent to Fremont. Before Yorktown we had lost two other divisions under McDowell. We had since left garrisons in Yorktown, Gloucester and Williamsburg. We had lost men under fire and by disease, as well as by straggling. Nothing came to fill up the gaps. When an American regiment marches to the war it goes as a whole, and leaves behind it no depots of recruits to restore its ranks as they are wasted away.

It will be easily seen how much reason we had to be anxious about this diminution of the army, while we knew that the confederates were steadily swelling their force, and while by plunging more deeply into the heart of the enemy's country we were daily moving further from our own base of operations, and losing at once the moral and material aid of the navy, the coöperation of which had hitherto proved so powerful and so useful.

I am aware that the evacuation of Norfolk was followed by

an important event of good augury to the federal cause. The *Merrimac*, which was no longer commanded by the brave Buchanan, and which had now no place of refuge, was burned by her new captain. Henceforth James river was opened to the federals, but unfortunately it was opened just too late. The iron-clad gunboats Galena, Naugatuck and Monitor, ran up to within seven miles of Richmond: there they found the river barred by a stockade which could not be forced, and its lofty banks defended by a battery of heavy guns, which could not be silenced. The great gun of the Naugatuck burst: the Monitor could not give her cannon elevation enough to reach the batteries of "Fort Darling." As to the Galena, her cuirass, three inches and a half thick, failed to protect her against conical 100-pounders, and she was forced to retire, after a heroic fight, with a large number of her crew placed *hors du combat*. A land attack upon the forts was found to be necessary, if the passage was to be forced; but in the face of the confederates, massed at a short distance before Richmond, such an operation could only have been attempted by the whole army. To accomplish it, the moment the news of the destruction of the Merrimac reached General McClellan, he should have abandoned the plan of campaign which he had begun to execute, and sought the James river by a rapid oblique march, in order to combine his operations with those of the navy upon that river. To-day, with the added experience of the events which actually occurred, I am inclined to think this would have been a wiser course to pursue. Of course, the passage from the Pamunkey to the James would have been dangerous; the passage of the lower Chickahominy, or of the Lower James, according as it might have been determined upon to operate up the right or up the left bank of the latter river, would have been a difficult and delicate thing to attempt, with the grand army of the confederates hanging upon the flank of the federals. Yet this risk would have been better than the dismal position in which the army really found itself for a month in the marshes of the Chickahominy. But who could at that time have foreseen, that at the decisive moment of the campaign, inundations unexampled at that season of the year would thwart the efforts and paralyze the movements of the Potomac army, as they did on the day of the battle of Fair Oaks? Or who, again, could foresee that the 80,000 men, assembled before Washington, would do nothing, and less than nothing, to aid the army in overcoming the concentration of forces it was called upon to encounter?

We continued, then, our forward movement, and notwithstanding the almost constant rains, we were not long reaching the banks of the Chickahominy, at a place called Bottom Bridge, ten miles from Richmond, where the York river railroad, which we had been following from White House, crosses the river on a bridge temporarily destroyed by the enemy. Here we were fairly at the gates of Richmond. Down to this time the campaign, if it had not been brilliant, had at least been fertile in results. Yorktown, one of the most important military positions of the enemy, had fallen. Norfolk, the magnificent arsenal from which the South drew the greater part of its military stores had been abandoned, and the necessity of abandoning it had brought on the destruction of the formidable Merrimac. Finally, General McClellan had succeeded in pitching his camp without accident in front of the capital of the Seceded States, and of their main army. The confederates could fall back no further, without losing all their prestige in the eyes of their partisans, and of the whole world. They were thus driven to accept a decisive battle upon this point. In our actual circumstances, it was no slight merit to have forced an adversary back upon such a necessity. I know that a battle ought to have been won at this point, and that it was not won. But the whole responsibility of this matter by no means rests upon the General or upon his army.

Who were the men, who by driving him into an untimely campaign, had revealed to the enemy operations not yet ripe for execution? Was McClellan responsible for that want of unity in the ends and in the action of the government which had trammelled the movements of the army since he had been deprived of the chief command and supreme directions of the forces? Was McClellan responsible for the systematic diminution of his forces, which, in the face of the agglomeration of the forces of the enemy, had successively deprived him, since the campaign had opened, of the division of Blenker and of two-thirds of McDowell's corps, without sending him one solitary man to fill up the gaps made by sickness and by the cannon? In spite of all these obstacles he had reached the walls of Richmond, but he had no longer the means of striking the great blow which probably would have ended the war. In a hostile country covered with forests, where one sees nothing and knows little, what appears a simple reconnoissance may often prove a serious and general attack. There a large force is needed to guard against surprises, and a still larger force to secure lines of communication, which cannot be broken without danger.

Evidently we needed reinforcements. Could we obtain them? Could the federals meet, with a powerful concentration of troops, that concentration which the enemy had effected, and to the reality of which the observations of our aeronauts, as well as the statements of deserters, daily bore witness? This was the first question we had to ask ourselves. General Wool from Norfolk, Burnside from North Carolina, might send some men, but very few, while around Washington more than eighty thousand were collected. Of these about one-half were making head against the partisan Jackson in the valley of the Shenandoah. The rest were collected under McDowell at Fredericksburg, sixty miles to the north of Richmond. They had rebuilt the railway bridge over the

Rappahannock, and in three or four days they might have joined the army of McClellan. They covered nothing at Fredericksburg, and were so notoriously useless to the federal cause that in the confederate journals they were spoken of as the "fifth wheel of the coach." It was known that McDowell desired ardently to give the lie to these railleries by bringing at the decisive moment his assistance to the cause of the Union. Accordingly McClellan had no sooner arrived before Richmond than he undertook to discover what he had to hope for from this quarter. No official advices, either from Washington or from Fredericksburg, had informed him of McDowell's presence at that point, only sixty miles distant, but rumor and probability agreed so well in placing him there that the General-in-Chief resolved to make an attempt to establish communication with him. On the night of the 26th he sent forward General Porter's division with a few squadrons of cavalry, in a furious storm, to Hanover Court House, a village about twenty miles north of Richmond, where the railway to Fredericksburg crosses the Pamunkey. The troops of Porter moved rapidly, and about midday on the 27th came upon the hostile division of Branch, at Hanover Court House. This they assailed with vigor, dispersed it, and took one of its guns. Assailed in their turn by confederate troops who had suffered them to pass by the woods in which they lay hidden, the federals turned on their new enemies and scattered them also. This brilliant affair cost the federals 400 men, and left General Porter in possession of a cannon, of 500 prisoners, and of two bridges, one on the Fredericksburg and one on the Virginia Central road. The advanced guard of McDowell was then at Bowling Green, fifteen miles from that of Porter. It needed only an effort of the will; the two armies were united, and the possession of Richmond certain! Alas! this effort was not made. I cannot recall those fatal moments without a real sinking of the heart. Seated in an orchard in the bivouac of Porter, amid the joyous excitement which follows a successful combat, I saw the Fifth Cavalry bring in whole companies of confederate prisoners, with arms and baggage, their officers at their head. But neither the glad confidence of the federals nor the discouragement of their enemies deceived me, and I asked myself how many of these gallant young men who surrounded me, relating their exploits of the day before, would pay with their lives for the fatal error which was on the point of being committed. Not only did not the two armies unite, but the order came from Washington to burn the bridges which had been seized. This was the clearest way of saying to the Army of the Potomac, and to its chiefs, that in no case could they count on the support of the armies of Upper Virginia.

This unfortunate step had been taken upon hearing of the successful dash which the confederate General Jackson was then making upon the Upper Potomac. This skillful leader ascertaining that the federal forces in that region were broken up into a number of small independent corps, under the orders of Generals Fremont, Banks, Shields and others, had taken advantage of this state of anarchy to give them battle one after another. He had driven Banks across the Potomac and had created such confusion that he was supposed to be on the point of entering Washington. With more than 40,000 men to defend that city, with the easily tenable line of the Potomac, and the vast entrenched camp which surrounds the Capital it was not thought to be safe. McDowell was summoned in hot haste to join in the pursuit of Jackson. McDowell, as was to have been expected, arrived too late. But the bridges which might have connected his operations with those of McClellan, had been destroyed. It is probable that in the confusion which reigned at Washington, the order to destroy them was sent for the purpose of preventing the confederates from using them to send reinforcements to Jackson.

But let us turn from this afflicting spectacle; let us turn from Jackson playing at fast and loose with the four Generals opposed to him. He had carried his point. His daring movement had prevented the junction of McDowell with McClellan, at the moment when that junction would have been decisive of the campaign. Henceforth the Army of the Potomac could rely only upon itself. No time was to be lost before acting, for every day augmented the disproportion between the forces of the adversaries, and it was to be feared the federals encamped amid the marshes of the Chickahominy would suffer severely from the great heats now setting in. We had been for some days face to face. The federal advance was but five miles distant from Richmond. Skirmishes were of daily occurrence, and with the feeling on both sides a general action was inevitable. General McClellan waited for two things before making the attack. He waited for the roads which the rain had swamped to become solid and practicable for his artillery, and for the completion of the numerous bridges which he was throwing over the Chickahominy.

The character of the localities, the impossibility of quitting the railway by which the army was supplied, and the necessity of keeping on his guard against any attempt of the enemy to turn his position, had forced the General to divide his troops into two wings on the opposite banks of the river. It was consequently most important to be able to mass them rapidly, either on the right bank for an offensive movement against Richmond, or on the left bank against any attempt to turn the position. The latter danger was much to be feared, for the confederates had retained possession of several bridges on the upper Chickahominy, which would permit them to occupy the excellent positions that are to be found on the left bank, just so soon as the northern army should abandon these positions. In this way they would have shut us up upon the right bank, blockaded, starved, and reduced to an extremely critical condition. Unfortunately everything dragged with us. The roads were long in drying, the bridges were long in building. "Never have we seen so rainy a season," said the oldest inhabitant. "Never did we see bridges so difficult to build," said the engineers. The abominable river laughed at all their efforts. Too narrow for a bridge of boats, too deep and too muddy for piers, here a simple brook some ten yards wide, flowing betwen two plains of quicksand in which the horses sank up to the girths and which offered no bearings—there divided into a thousand tiny rivulets spread over a surface of three hundred yards and traversing one of those wooded morasses which are peculiar to tropical countries, changing its level and its bed from day to day, the river in its capricious and uncertain sway annulled and undid to-day the labors of yesterday, carried on under a burning sun and often under the fire of the enemy. And so went by days upon days, precious irrecoverable days! Perhaps, let us frankly say it, the army was not so eager to act as it ought to have been. To advance and meet the enemy upon his own ground was an adventurous enterprise somewhat foreign to an American army. In that country men affect the slow, circumspect, methodical kind of war which leaves nothing to chance. This delay, as we have already remarked, is part of the national character; it is, also, to a certain extent, imposed upon the generals by the nature of their troops. These troops are very brave, but as we have attempted to show, it follows from the weakness of the hierarchical bond among them that one can never be sure that they will do exactly what they are ordered to do. Individual wills, as capricious as popular majorities, play too great a part among them. The leader has to turn his head to see if his men are following him. He is not certain that his subordinates are attached to him by the ties of discipline and duty. Hence, hesitation, and with it conditions unfavorable to any dashing enterprise. "If we could but be attacked and have a defensive battle," I often heard it said, "the day would be half won." This wish was granted. The enemy was the first to attack. On the 31st of May he put an end to all uncertainties and speculations as to the best way of getting at him by throwing himself boldly, with all his forces, upon the army of the Potomac. The bloody conflict which raged on that day and the next has received the name of the battle of Fair Oaks.

At the time when this attack was made, the federal army occupied a position in the form of a letter V. The base of the V rests upon Bottom Bridge, where the railway crosses the Chickahominy. The left arm follows this railway and the Williamsburg road towards Richmond. Here lay the left wing, formed of four divisions, echelonned one behind the other, between Savage's Station and Fair Oaks, and encamped in the woods on either side of the railway. The right arm of the V follows the left bank of the river. Here lay the right wing, consisting of five divisions and the reserves. To pass from one end to the other of these two wings, one must have crossed the river at Bottom Bridge, and the distance would have been something like 15 miles. As the crow flies, the distance, on the contrary, was small, but the Chickahominy flowed between the two arms of the V. It was to unite these two arms that three or four bridges across the river were commenced, one alone of which was fit for use on May 31st. It had been built by General Sumner, about half way between Bottom Bridge and the most advanced point of the federal lines. It saved that day the whole federal army from destruction. The other bridges were ready, but could not be thrown across the stream. This fact saved the Confederate army.

The strength of the enemy was thrown against the left wing. The advance of this wing lay at Fair Oaks, a station on the York river road, and at Seven Pines, a point on the

Williamsburg road. Here the federals had thrown up a redoubt in a clearing, where there were a few houses, and they had felled trees to widen the sweep of their guns. The rest of the country was one dense wood. The evening before we had a terrific storm, with torrents of rain; the roads were frightful.

Suddenly, about 1 P. M., the weather being grey and dull, we heard a very lively fire of musketry. The pickets and the advance were violently driven in; the woods around Fair Oaks and Seven Pines were filled with hostile sharpshooters. The troops flew to arms and fought desperately; but the forces of the enemy constantly increased, and he was not checked by his losses. The redoubt at Seven Pines was surrounded, and its defenders fell valiantly. Here, among others, Colonel Bailey, of the artillery, met a glorious death among his guns. The redoubt was carried, and the Northern troops fell into some confusion. In vain did Generals Keyes and Naglee make a thousand efforts to rally their troops; they were wholly disregarded. At this moment they perceived a small battalion of French troops, known as the "Gardes Lafayette," standing in good order. The Generals rode up to it, put themselves at its head, charged the enemy, and retook a battery. The battalion lost a fourth of its numbers in this charge, but like genuine Frenchmen, the same all the world over, they cried—"They may call us *Gardes Lafourchette* now, if they like," in allusion to an uncomplimentary nickname which had been bestowed on them.

Meanwhile Heintzelman advanced to the rescue with his two divisions. As at Williamsburg, so here, Kearney came up at the right moment to restore the battle. Berry's brigade of this division, made up of Michigan regiments, and of an Irish battalion, advances as firm as a stone wall, through the disordered masses which are wavering upon the battle field, and does more, by its single example, than the strongest reinforcements. Nearly a mile of ground had been lost, fifteen guns, and the divisional camp of Casey in the advance. But now the troops began to stand firm. A sort of line of battle was formed across the woods, perpendicularly to the railway and to the road, and there the repeated assaults of the enemy are met. The left cannot be turned, being protected by the impenetrable morasses of White Oak Swamp; but the right might be surrounded. At this very moment, indeed, a strong confederate column is moving in that direction. If it succeed in getting between Bottom Bridge and the federal troops who are fighting at Savage's Station, the whole left wing is lost. It will have no retreat left, and must be overwhelmed. But exactly at this moment (six o'clock P. M.), new actors come upon the stage. Sumner, who has at last passed the river with Sedgwick's division on the bridge built by his troops, and who, with a soldier's instinct, has marched straight to the cannon through the woods, suddenly appears upon the flank of the hostile column which is trying to cut off Heintzelman and Keyes. He plants in a clearing a battery which he has succeeded in bringing up. His guns are not rifled guns, the rage of the hour, and fit only to be fired in cool blood, and at long range in an open country; they are real fighting guns, old twelve-pound howitzers carrying either a round projectile, which ricochets and rolls, or a good dose of grape. The simple and rapid fire of these pieces makes terrible havoc in the hostile ranks. In vain Johnston sends up his best troops against this battery, the flower of South Carolina, including the Hampton Legion; in vain does he come upon the field in person; nothing can shake the federal ranks. When night falls, it was the federals who, bayonet in hand, and gallantly led by Sumner himself, charged furiously upon the foe, and drove him before them with fearful slaughter, as far as Fair Oaks station.

Night put an end to the conflict. On either side no one

knew anything more of the result of the fighting than his own eyes had seen. Friends and foes flinging themselves down in the woods lay there, among heaps of the dead and the dying, wherever the darkness found them. The fatigue of this obstinate fight, as well as the shades of night, had brought about one of those tacit truces not uncommon in war.

Evidently Johnston had imagined that by throwing his whole force on the four federal divisions which had crossed the Chickahominy he could crush them before the rest of the army could come to their assistance. For the moment he had failed, thanks to the energetic resistance of these divisions and to the furious and unexpected onslaught of the troops of Sumner. No doubt he counted upon the tremendous storm of the previous night to swell the Chickahominy so as to make it impossible to throw any bridge over the river, and to carry away with its flood any bridge already fixed. But the capricious stream undid his combinations, as a few hours later it undid those of his enemies. The effect of the deluge of rain was not immediate. Twenty-four hours passed before it was fully felt. Was the interval employed as profitably as it ought to have been by the federals? This is a question which will always afford a matter of controversy, like so many similar questions which inevitably arise out of the history of most great battles. It was not till one in the afternoon that the battle began. Some time had been lost under the impression that the attack on the right bank might be a feint to draw over the federal troops while the main body of the confederates was preparing to debouch upon the left bank. An end was soon put to all doubts on the subject by the vehemence of the attack, and by the aeronauts who reported the whole confederate army moving to the scene of action. It was then that Sumner received the order to pass the river with his divisions. He executed it rapidly, marching a little at haphazard at the head of his column with no other guide than the cannonade, and arrived at the critical hour and at the critical place. Some persons thought then, and think still that if instead of Sumner alone, all the divisions of the right wing had been ordered to cross the river the order could have been executed. It is easy to see what must have happened, if instead of 15,000, 50,000 men had been thrown upon Johnston's flank. But Sumner's bridge, no doubt, would not have sufficed for the passage of such a force. At midnight the rear of his column was still struggling slowly to cross this rude structure against all the difficulties of a roadway formed of trunks which slipped and rolled under the horses' feet, of a muddy morass at either end, and of a pitchy dark night rendered darker still by the density of the forest. But several other bridges were ready to be thrown across at other points. Not a moment should have been lost in fixing them, and no regard should have been paid to the efforts of the enemy to prevent this from being done. Johnston had paraded a brigade ostentatiously as a sort of scare-crow at the points which were most fitting for this enterprise; but the stake was so vast, the result to be sought after so important, the occasion so unexpected and so favorable for striking a decisive blow, that in our judgment nothing should have prevented the army from attempting this operation at every risk. Here again it paid the penalty of that American tardiness which is more marked in the character of the army than in that of its leader. It was not till seven in the evening that the resolution was taken of throwing over all the bridges and passing the whole army over by daybreak to the right bank. It was too late. Four hours had been lost, and the opportunity, that moment which is ever more fugitive in war than in any other occupation of life, had taken wing. The flood on which Johnston had vainly counted and which had not interfered with the passage of Sumner, came on in the night. The river suddenly rose two feet and continued to rise very rapidly, carrying away the new bridges, lifting and sweeping away the trees which formed the floor of Sumner's bridge, and covering the valley with its unruly waters. Nothing could cross over. With the first light of day the battle began again fiercely on the left bank. The enemy came on in masses without order or method, and fell upon the federals, who feeling their inferiority in numbers, and having no hope of succor, attempted to do nothing more than to hold their own. The fight raged on either side with savage energy. There was no shouting or noise. When either party was too hard pressed it took to the bayonet. The artillery from beyond the clearing sent its shells over the combatants. Ah! I wish that all those who careless of the past and urged on by I know not what selfish calculations, have lavished their encouragements upon this fatal slaveholders' rebellion, could have looked in person upon this fratricidal strife. I could have asked that as a just punishment they should be condemned to gaze upon that fearful battle-field where the dead and the dying were piled up by thousands. I could have wished them to see the thousand ambulances hastily assembled around those scattered houses. What varieties of misery and of anguish! There was something particularly horrible in the ambulances. The houses were too few to contain even a small minority of the wounded, and they had necessarily been heaped up around the field; but although they uttered no complaints and bore their fate with the most stoical courage, their exposure under the noonday sun of a burning June soon became intolerable; and then they were to be seen, gathering up what little strength was left to them, crawling about in search of a little shade. I shall never forget a rose-bush in full bloom, the perfumed flowers of which I was admiring while I talked with a friend, when he pointed out to me under the foliage one of these poor creatures who had just drawn his last breath. We looked at one another in silence, our hearts filled with the most painful emotions. Sad scenes, from which the pen of the writer, like the eye of the spectator, hastens to turn away!

Towards noon the firing gradually slackened and ceased. The enemy was retreating, but the federals were in no condition to pursue him. We did not then know how severe a loss the confederates had suffered, in the person of their leader, Johnston, grievously wounded. It was mainly to his absence that we must attribute the disconnected character of the attack made upon the federals in the morning. When the firing ceased at noon, the confederates, we were told, (for amid those immense forests we heard nothing and must divine everything,) were in a state of inextricable confusion. What might not have happened, if at this moment the 35,000 fresh troops on the other bank of the Chickahominy could have appeared upon the flank of this disordered army, after passing the bridges in safety!

Such is the story of this singular battle, which, complicated as it was by incidents beyond human control, may yet, I think, be taken as a fair type of American battles.* The conflict had been sanguinary, since the Northern army had lost 5,000, and the Southern at least 8,000 men. But the results to either party were negative. The confederates, much superior in numbers, had made a vigorous attack, had driven back their adversaries about a mile, had captured several cannon and had stopped there, satisfied with earning thus the right to sing the song of victory.

The federals had had the defensive battle which they desired, had repulsed the enemy, taken a General and many prisoners; but arrested by natural obstacles which perhaps were not wholly insurmountable, they had gained nothing by their success.

* I cannot refrain from mentioning here a most characteristic incident: newspaper venders were crying the latest New York papers on the battle-field during the battle, and they found buyers.

In point of fact, both sides had failed for want of organization, for want of hierarchy, for the want of the bond which hierarchy creates between the soul of the General and the great body called an army, that powerful bond which suffers a Commander to demand and to obtain from the blind confidence of his troops, those extraordinary efforts by which battles are won. Nevertheless, although the losses of the enemy were the larger, the check which the federals had received was especially disastrous to them. They had missed an unique opportunity of striking a decisive blow.

These opportunities never returned; and moreover, in the then circumstances of the federals, time was working against them.

V.

The Seven Days' Battles.

The day after this battle, McClellan recovered, without a blow, the stations of Fair Oaks and Seven Pines, so that the armies were once more in the same positions as before. For nearly a month they looked each other in the face, in a state of inaction which yet was not repose. On the contrary, this month, with its overwhelming alternations of heat and rain, with the immense labors imposed upon the soldiers, with its never-ending alarms and partial combats, was a dreary and a trying season.

The federal army neither wished to offer, nor to invite another such battle as that of Fair Oaks till its bridges should be built, and its two wings put into communication with each other. Diluvian rains were in the way of the result. Moreover, we had profited by past experience, and we wished to give these bridges, together with a monumental solidity, an extent of space which should traverse not only the river, but the whole valley. If we did this, we should have nothing more to fear from inundations, but to do this required much time and many efforts. When it was completed, the left wing remained exposed to an attack from the whole confederate force; so we hastened to entrench ourselves along our whole line. This was a tremendous piece of work. As in all other places, redoubts and embankments had to be raised, rifle-pits had to be dug, and all this under a broiling sun. We had furthermore to cut down the trees on the site selected, and for several hundred yards in advance. In some places no earth-works were erected, but it was thought sufficient to cut down the forest into the contour of a regular fortification. The thickest part of the woods left standing and salient in the midst of a vast abattis, played the part of a bastion. The artillery and the sharpshooters, placed in this wood, flanked with their fire the hedges which represented the curtains.

The defenders of these new-fashioned works, it is true, had no other protection against the hostile fire than the foliage, through which it was impossible to draw a direct aim upon them.

All these labors were executed with admirable energy and intelligence. In this aspect the American soldier has no rival; patient of fatigue, rich in resources, he is an excellent digger and ditcher, an excellent woodman, a good carpenter, and even something of a civil engineer. Often in the course of the campaign we came upon a flour mill or a saw mill, turned sometimes by a water wheel, sometimes by an engine, which the enemy as he retired had thrown out of order. You were sure to find immediately in the first regiment that came up men who could repair, refit, and set them going again for the service of the army. But nothing was so remarkable as to see a detail fall to work at making an abattis in the woods. It is impossible to give an idea of the celerity with which work of this kind was done. I remember to have seen a grove a hundred acres in extent, of ancestral oaks and other hard wood trees cut down in a single day by a single battalion. Nevertheless, all this work was not done without much fatigue both moral and material, as the natural consequence of incessant toil under an incessant fire.

In these vast and pathless woods, where you run a constant risk of being surprised, it is impossible to throw out one's advance very far. So we form what in America is called a "picket line," an uninterrupted line of sentinels supported by strong reserves, which never move far from the corps to which they belong. The two armies were now so near together, and so determined to cede no inch of ground that their pickets were stationed within hailing distance of one another. Generally they got along very amicably together, and contented themselves with a reciprocal watchfulness. Sometimes friendly communications took place between them—they trafficked in various trifles, and exchanged the Richmond newspapers for the New York Herald. It even happened one day that some federal officers were invited by their confederate comrades to a ball in Richmond, on condition that they would suffer their eyes to be bandaged in going and returning. But a single shot would disturb these good relations—the firing would last a greater part of an hour, and a hundred men perhaps be killed or wounded before they became quiet again.

At other times the troops were surprised in their tents by a shower of shells, coming nobody knew where from, over the heads of the pickets. This was a disagreeable *reveilleé* when it happened at night. If it took place in the daytime the men would clamber up into some high tree to spy out the spot from which the firing came. This would be betrayed by the smoke, and sometimes a confederate soldier would be seen perched in some towering tree himself directing the fire of the artillerymen. Then the federals would reply, and make great efforts to "bring down" the aerial gunner. These isolated annoyances, whether of "picket firing" or "long-range shelling" troubled nobody but the troops immediately exposed. They were happening at every hour of the day, and there is nothing which may not become a habit. But sometimes the musketry and the cannon came booming together with a vivacity which no one could mistake, and then every one sprang to arms, and the staff got into the saddle. The enemy was making a demonstration in force, and we were replying. Would a battle grow out of it?

This constant uncertainty was singularly exhausting. But the battle never came. The Southern generals were no more anxious than the Northern to bring on prematurely a general engagement. They had their plans, and were leaving them to ripen. Every day brought them new reinforcements, and they expected still more. The whole force of the rebellion must soon be gathered in upon Richmond. Meanwhile, disease ravaged the exhausted soldiers of the federal army. The extreme heat combined with the marshy exhalations generated fevers which took upon them almost instantly a typhoid character. Certain divisions which had already been weakened in action had two thousand sick upon their list. A system of temporary and irregular leaves of absence had grown up in the army, which also conspired to reduce its effective strength. Many colonels arrogated to themselves the right of granting leaves of absence for a few days to soldiers who went and were seen no more.

It is right, however, to say that at this critical time General McClellan received some small reinforcements. One of his old divisions, that of McCall, was restored to him. Moreover, Fortress Monroe having been at last put under his orders, he had drawn thence some 5 or 6,000 men. This was something, but it was not enough; it was far from being enough to fill up the gaps made in the ranks, which widened daily.

These days of inaction had a further disadvantage, that they encouraged hostile partisans to dashing enterprises. The feat undertaken by the confederate Colonel Lee was one of the most singular episodes of the war. At the head of 1,500 horsemen he attacked some squadrons which were patrolling at Hanover Court House, dispersed them and made a successful inroad upon the communications of the army. His project was to cut off the York river railway, under cover of the night; but it did not succeed. We, however, had the singular exhibition of a combat between cavalry and a railway train; the train literally charging both the hostile cavalry and the obstructions placed on the track, escaped with the loss of a few men killed and wounded by the fire of the enemy. But if Colonel Lee failed to destroy the railway, he made a brilliant *razzia* upon the army stores, and escaped without damage to himself. The real mischief done was that attempts of this sort might be constantly renewed, and that we had not troops enough to oppose them everywhere at once.

Although under all these trials the *morale* of the army continued to be excellent,* it was impossible not to see that the expedition was in a critical situation, which was daily growing worse. Having lost fully one-third of its numbers during the campaign, decimated by disease and threatened in the rear, the army found itself in the heart of the insurgent territory, menaced by forces twice or thrice more numerous than itself. It was impossible to think of remaining idle in front of the enemy as had been done during the winter at Washington and more recently at Corinth. This General McClellan felt; and as soon as the bridges were fixed he determined to

* I hardly know whether I ought to mention among other causes which might have affected this *morale* the disagreeable spectacle of the gigantic posters which an embalmer exhibited in the midst of the camp, and in which this tradesman, speculating at once upon the losses of the army and on the domestic affections of their friends, promised to embalm the slain and send them home at a reasonable rate. This enterprising rival of Gannal, by the way, saved the life of a colonel, who having been thrown into a prolonged swoon by the explosion of a shell, was supposed to be dead, and having been committed to the embalmer, recovered his consciousness during the operation.

act. A plan had been thought of by him; it was to transport the whole army seventeen miles from its position at that time, to abandon the line of communications on the York river, and to seek, with the assistance of the navy, a new base on the James river. If this movement could be successfully and secretly made, the chances of a great battle fought on the river bank with the coöperation of the gunboats covering one flank of the army, would be much more favorable to the federals; but the movement had dangers of its own, and it was not easy of accomplishment in the face of the enemy; not to mention the undesirableness of an apparent retreat.

The plan then was renounced, or at least adjourned. With American tenacity, a quality which is just as remarkable in the people as their habit of delay, and perhaps balances that habit, it was settled that the army should not fall back, unless it was absolutely driven so to do. The General wished to carry out the operations already commenced; but he nevertheless took the wise precaution of sending to City Point on the river James, vessels loaded with ammunition, provisions, and supplies of all sorts. This done, General McClellan devoted himself to bringing on a general action on the ground lying between himself and Richmond, a ground which he had carefully studied in numerous reconnoissances. These reconnoissances had given rise to a number of adventures. On one occasion the General had climbed with several of his officers, to the top of a high tree, and there, every man on his branch with spy-glass in hand, they had held a sort of council of war. This took place within a hundred paces of the hostile pickets, whom no attempt at observations could escape. We dreaded to hear the crack of the rifles of the famous Southern squirrel-shooters; but they were magnanimous, and the reconnoissance ended without a mishap. On another occasion, the staff of a confederate commander appeared simultaneously with our own upon the banks of the Chickahominy. At once the hostile gentlemen ordered up one of their bands, which played a popular air; but it was hardly ended before the musicians gave way to a battery, which, coming up at full gallop, opened a terrible fire, to which we soon responded. These examinations convinced us that the enemy was not idle, and that he had thrown up works, armed with heavy guns, precisely where we did not wish to see them. At last, after many experiments, the battle began. On the 25th of June, Hooker received his orders to advance a mile, to a large clearing on the direct road to Richmond. It was calculated that this movement would be followed by a general resistance on the part of the confederates, which would renew the battle of Fair Oaks, with the important difference that our bridges being all solidly established, we could command the assistance of the whole army.

If the challenge were not accepted, then we should have made one step forward; we should make another next day, and so, by degrees, we should enter Richmond. Moreover, we trusted to our star for the rest. Hooker, mounted on a white horse, which made him conspicuous in the woods to all of us and to the enemy, advanced gallantly. The ground he was to conquer was taken, lost, retaken and finally held by him, with a loss of from 400 to 500 men. His two brave brigadiers, Groves and Sickles, gave him the most energetic assistance; but during the conflict, serious news had reached us.

Deserters, runaway negroes, the Washington telegraph itself, generally so sober in its information, agreed in this news: numerous reinforcements had reached Richmond from the South. Beauregard, set free by the cessation of operations in the Southwest, had brought the aid of his capacity and of his prestige to the pro-slavery cause. Jackson, leaving the eighty thousand defenders of Washington breathless from their idle chase after him, had completed the concentration of the whole

Southern army. His advance was already at Hanover Court House, and his corps, increased by Whiting's division, was estimated at 30,000 men.

The federal attack upon Richmond could no longer be prosecuted; the presence of Jackson at Hanover Court House proved that he intended to attack our communications, and cut them off by seizing the York river railway. The manœuvre was soon put beyond a doubt. A considerable body of troops were seen to leave Richmond, move in the direction of Jackson, and execute that movement to turn us, the danger of which we have already pointed out. Profiting by his numerical superiority, the enemy offered us battle on both sides of the river at once.

All the chances of success were in his favor. Let the reader recall the figure V which we used in describing the battle of Fair Oaks. The situation of the army of McClellan is the same now as then, excepting that the two arms of the V are now connected by bridges, which offer all necessary facilities for transporting the different corps rapidly from one bank of the river to the other. The federal main body, composed of eight divisions, but considerably reduced in effective strength, is upon the left arm of the V—the right bank, that is, of the Chickahominy, and occupies the entrenchments which front Richmond. Before these troops lies the mass of the hostile army, also established in entrenched positions. Upon the right arm of the V, or the left bank of the river, lies the federal General Fitz John Porter, with two divisions and the regular reserves. Against him it was that Jackson marched with the corps of General Hill from Richmond, the whole being under the orders of General Lee, who had succeeded Johnston in the chief command.

Substantially, then, the Army of the Potomac was about to engage two armies each equal in force to itself. Battles have sometimes been won in such circumstances. But no one should count upon such favors from fortune. The best thing to be done was to get well out of so critical a position. There was nothing for it but to retreat promptly; unluckily, however, this was not to be so easily done. We had a choice of dangers. To concentrate on the left bank of the Chickahominy was to abandon the enterprise against Richmond, and to risk a disastrous retreat upon White House and Yorktown, with the whole confederate army at our heels, in a country where we could hope for no support. There was no good to be expected from this plan. To pass to the right bank was to risk the enemy's cutting our communications with White House, and seizing the railway which brought our supplies. We should then be forced to open new communications with the James river, and to move in that direction *en masse* and with no delay. This would be a retreat, but for a few miles only, and if we were but moderately reinforced, with the support of the navy, we could reassume the offensive either against Richmond itself, on the right bank of the river, or against Petersburg on the left, the fall of that place involving the fall of Richmond McClellan chose the latter course.

As we have said, he had long considered it as one of the necessities of his position, and had even taken some contingent steps in regard to it, the wisdom of which was about to be signally vindicated; but there was a vast difference between making this retreat at one's own time and by a free, spontaneous movement, and making it hastily under the threatening pressure of two hostile armies. But there was no time for deliberation. The resolution taken upon the spur of the moment must be carried at once into effect. The distance from Fair Oaks to the James river was not great; it was but seventeen miles. But the stores and baggage had to be moved upon a single road, exposed in front to the enemy, who by several different roads radiating from Richmond could throw a considerable force upon several different points at once. The speed with which the operation was conducted upset his calculations: he probably supposed that we should feel the ground before we acted, and perhaps he thought that McClellan would find it hard to make up his mind to abandon his lines at White House. He acted at least as if this were his view. The troops of General Hill, mentioned above, having crossed the Chickahominy at Meadow Bridge on the 26th, the day after the affair with Hooker, in the afternoon attacked the troops of McCall, the advance of Porter on the left bank. This first conflict was very severe; but McCall occupied a strong position at Beaver Dam, a sort of ravine bordered with beautiful catalpa trees, then in flower. There he had made abattis and thrown up some earth so that he could not be overcome, notwithstanding the length of the fight which lasted until nightfall. This vigorous resistance compelled the enemy to throw numerous reinforcements across the river. This was exactly what General McClellan desired. His intention was to fix the attention of the enemy here while on the right bank he prepared his movement to the James river.

The night was spent in passing over to this bank the whole of Porter's baggage and uniting it with the long train which was to set out in the evening of the 27th. The orders were given to re-embark or destroy all the stores and magazines along the railway to White House and to evacuate that depot. General Stoneman with a flying column was charged with the execution of this order. He was to delay the advance of the enemy and fall back when he had done his duty upon Yorktown. All this was carried out exactly. At daybreak on the 27th, McCall was ordered to fall back on the bridges thrown across the Chickahominy at Gaines's Mill. Followed up rapidly, as he had expected to be, he joined the other troops of Porter's corps, the division of Morell and the regulars commanded by General Sykes. Porter's duty, demanding as much self-possession as vigor, was to make a stand in front of the bridges in order to give the army time to accomplish its general movement. He was not to cross the bridges till the evening of the 27th, and was then to destroy them. His three divisions were attacked early in the day. The corps of Jackson coming in from Hanover Court House, took part in the action. The battle was fought in a rolling country, extensively wooded, but upon certain points open and cleared. The struggle was arduous; the federals resisted with success; there was even one moment at which Porter might have thought himself victorious. This would have been a great advantage, and might have profoundly modified the position. Accordingly, during this moment of hope, McClellan hastened to throw upon the left bank all the troops not absolutely necessary to guard the lines in front of Richmond. One division, that of Slocum, crossed the bridges before four o'clock and joined in the action. Another, Richardson's, reached the scene only at nightfall. At the moment when these reinforcements began to take part in the fight, the scene had an imposing character of grandeur. We had 35,000 men engaged, a part in the woods, a part in the plain, forming a line a mile and a half long. A numerous artillery thundered upon every side. In the valley of the Chickahominy the lancers with floating pennons were stationed as a reserve; and this whole animated picture of the battle was set in a picturesque landscape illuminated by the last rays of the sun going down below a horizon as crimson as blood. Suddenly the volleys became extraordinarily intense. The reserves, which had till now been lying in the hollows, were called up, excited by shouts, and sent into the woods. The musketry becomes more and more violent, and rolls away toward the left. There can no longer be any doubt that the enemy is making a final effort on that side. The reserves are all engaged, there is not a disposable man left. It is six o'clock, the daylight is fast disappearing; if the federal army can hold out an hour longer the battle is won, for at every other point the enemy has been repulsed, and Jackson, Hill, Lee, and Longstreet will have urged up their troops in vain. For lack of infantry, Porter has put three batteries *en potence* on his extreme left to support the troops who are there sustaining an unequal fight; but these troops have been in action since early morning, they are worn out, and have fired almost their last cartridge. Now in their turn come up the confederate reserves; they deploy regularly into line against the federal left which gives way, breaks and disbands. The disorder grows from point to point till it reaches the centre of the federal lines. There is no panic; the men do not fly in the wild excitement of fear; but deaf to every appeal, they march off deliberately, their muskets at the shoulder, like people who have had enough of it, and do not believe success possible. In vain do the generals, the officers of the staff, among them the Count of Paris and the Duke of Chartres, ride sword in hand into the mélee to stop their disorderly movement; the battle of Gaines's Mill is lost. There is nothing left but to prevent a rout. The enemy, indeed, was advancing on the plain still in the same order, his infantry deployed by regiments *en echelon*, and every minute he was closing in upon the confused masses of the federals. Such is the fury of the cannonade and the musketry fire that the cloud of dust struck up from the ground floats steadily over the battle. Then came the order for the cavalry to charge. I happened at this moment to be near its position. I saw the troopers draw their swords with the sudden and electrical impulse of determination and devotion. As they got into motion, I asked a young officer the name of his regiment. "The Fifth cavalry," he replied, brandishing his sabre with a soldier's pride in his regiment. Unfortunate young man! I saw the same regiment next day. From the charge of that evening but two officers had returned. He was not one of them.

The charge failed against the dense battalions of the enemy, and the broken regiments galloping through the artillery and the flying infantry in the clouds of dust only increased the general disorder. The artillery horses were killed, and I saw, with painful emotion, the men working with the courage of desperation at guns which could no longer be removed. They dropped one after another. Two alone were left at last, and they continued to load and fire almost at point blank range upon the enemy. Then the deepening twilight hid the scene. All these guns were lost.

General Butterfield had made in vain the most superhuman efforts to save them. On foot, his horse having been shot, struck in the hat by the fragment of a shell, and his sabre hit by a ball, surrounded by his aids-de-camp, of whom several fell at his side, he had tried to rally the infantry around a flag planted in the ground. He succeeded, but only for a few moments; the precipitate rush of the retreat carried everything away. Happily, night came on, and after losing a mile of ground, the army reached the fresh brigades of Meagher and French, which were formed in good order. These brigades sent up a vigorous hurrah, and a few guns put anew in battery opened their fire upon the enemy, who paused at last, checked by this final and determined resistance.

As the last guns of this action were firing, we heard a lively rattle of musketry from the direction of Fair Oaks, on the other side of the river. It came from the confederates who were attacking the federal works; but the attack, which was probably only a demonstration, was vigorously repelled.

The day had been severe. In the main battle, that of Gaines's Mill, 35,000 federals had failed to defeat 60,000 confederates, but they had held them in check. More could not have been expected.

During the night the federals repassed the bridges of the Chickahominy in perfect order, destroying them after they had passed. They left behind them the field of battle, covered with the dead (for in this fierce conflict the losses on both sides had been considerable) a great number of wounded, too much hurt to be moved, a dozen guns, and a few prisoners, among whom was General Reynolds. The corps of Keyes, which was in the advance, fell back also towards James river, and took possession of the passage of a large morass, White Oak Swamp, which is traversed by the road the army was to take as well as by the principal lines of communication which could be used by the enemy to harass us.

The 28th and 29th of June were passed in sending forward the train of five thousand wagons, the siege train, a herd of twenty-five hundred oxen, and other *impedimenta.* The reader may judge what a piece of work this was, when he reflects that it was all to be done upon a single narrow road. The first day we were undisturbed; the enemy was exhausted by the previous day's battle; he seemed, moreover, astonished and disconcerted, and did not yet fully understand the object of the federal army. The whole of this army was united on the right bank of the Chickahominy, whilst the bulk of the confederate forces was upon the left bank, and the bridges were down. To recross the river, they would be forced either to build new bridges or to fall back some distance to the Mechanicsville bridge; either of which operations involved time. Now, time was everything, and the retreating army put it to good use. It was not until the 29th that the southern columns came in sight of the federal rear-guard. A battle at once began, at Savage's Station, but the enemy were vigorously received, and after repulsing them the federals waited till nightfall before recommencing their march. The last duty done by the telegraph the day before was to inform us that the confederates were at White House. This post they had found abandoned. The morning of the 29th had been spent by us in destroying all that could not be carried away from the camps. A complete railway train, locomotive, tender, and cars, which had been left on the rails was sent headlong over the broken bridge into the river. Nothing was left for the foe but three siege guns which could not be moved, and which we neglected to bury. These were the only siege guns he captured, although the story has been everywhere repeated that he took the whole federal siege train with the exception of these three pieces. The whole of that train reached the James river in safety. Our great misfortune was, that we were obliged to abandon so many of our wounded, not only at Gaines's Mill and at Savage's Station, but along the whole line of retreat. This misfortune was inevitable. It was only by ceaseless fighting that we could protect our retreat, and the transportation of so many wounded men would have required conveniences which we did not possess.

General McClellan, during the 29th, and the morning of the 30th, remained near White Oak Swamp, urging on the passage of his enormous train. The heat was overwhelming. His aids-de-camp, continually galloping from the rear-guard to the advance, were utterly exhausted. So long as this huge train divided the different parts of the army we were in great danger. But nothing disturbed the serene self-possession of the General-in-Chief. On the 29th, he had stopped, I remember, to rest in the verandah of a house by the way side, when the mistress of the establishment came to complain to him that the soldiers were eating her cherries. The General rose with a smile, went himself and put a stop to the pillage. But he could not prevent the shells, next day, from setting fire to the house of his pretty hostess.

At daybreak on the 30th McClellan had the satisfaction of seeing all his troops and all his trains in safety beyond White Oak Swamp which was to oppose a new barrier to the pursuit of the enemy. By the evening of the next day Generals Keyes and Porter were in communication with the gunboats on the James. The trains had moved upon roads pointed out by the negro guides. The heads of the columns had met nothing but small detachments of cavalry, which they had easily dispersed. The hardest part of the work was done, but it was to be supposed that the enemy would renew his attempt to disturb the retreat. So the General took his measures in time. He left Sumner and Franklin to act as the rear-guard, and hold the passage of White Oak Swamp; and put Heintzelman with the divisions of Hooker, Kearney, Sedgwick and McCall, across the point of intersection of the roads leading from Richmond. They protected the trains and reached the James river at the exact moment when the transports with provision and ammunition, and the hospital ships which with wise foresight General McClellan had ordered up ten days before, arrived from Fortress Monroe.

Meanwhile, as had been expected, Franklin and Sumner were sharply attacked in White Oak Swamp, to which point the confederate Generals had brought a large force of artillery. They fell back step by step. Later in the day Heintzelman also was attacked at the Cross-roads. Here, the battle raged with varying fortune, in the woods. The division of McCall suffered severely, and its commander was made prisoner; but Hooker and Kearney, coming to his help repulsed the assailants with great loss. They did not however, succeed in rescuing the General, who was sent into Richmond to join Reynolds.

Finally, a third attack upon the corps of Fitz-John Porter failed utterly under the combined fire of the field artillery, and the gunboats. Porter occupied a superb position at a place called Turkey Bend, by some persons, and Malvern Hill by others. This position was a lofty open plateau sloping gradually down to the roads by which the enemy must debouch. The left rested upon the river, where lay the Galena, the Monitor, and the flotilla of gunboats. The federal army then had nothing to fear from this side, and had consequently only one flank to protect, which was easily done with abattis and field works. On the evening of the 30th all the divisions of the army were united in this strong position, and here the whole train including the siege guns was sheltered. The army was in communication with its transports and supplies. The grand and daring movement by which it had escaped a serious danger and changed an untenable base of operations for one more safe and sure, had been accomplished; but after so prolonged an effort the troops were worn out; for five days they had been incessantly marching and fighting. The heat had added to their excessive fatigue; many men had been sun struck; others quitted the ranks and fell into the lamentable procession of sick and wounded which followed the army as well as it could, and as fast as it could. Doubtless during this difficult retreat, there had been moments of confusion and disorder, but of what army in like circumstances would not this have been true? This one fact remained unassailable; that attacked in the midst of a difficult and hostile country by twice its own force, the Army of the Potomac had succeeded in gaining a position in which it was out of danger, and from which, had it been properly reinforced, had the concentration of the enemy's forces been met by a like concentration, it might have rapidly resumed the offensive.

As we have said, each of its necessarily scattered sections had for five days been called upon to resist the most furious assaults and had done so with vigor. Now that it was assembled as a whole upon Malvern Hill the confederate army also reunited might possibly make a last effort against it. So in the night of the 30th of June and 1st of July McClellan prepared himself for this eventuality. He put his whole artillery, at least three hundred guns, into battery along the heights arranging them in such wise that their fire should not interfere with the defence by the infantry of the sort of glacis up which the enemy would be obliged to advance to the attack. The artillery fire was to be reinforced by the 100-pounders of the gunboats which were ordered to flank the position. It was mere madness to rush upon such obstacles; but the confederates attempted it. Again and again during the day of the 1st of July they undertook to carry Malvern Hill, but without the slightest chance of success. The whole day for them was an idle butchery. Their loss was very heavy; that of the federals insignificant. This success was due to two causes. First, to the fortunate foresight of the General, who, in spite of numerous natural obstacles to the passage of artillery, had spared nothing to bring his on, and next to the firmness of his troops. Men do not make such a campaign, and go through such experience as they had endured, without coming out more or less formed to war. If their primitive organization had been better, the survivors of this rude campaign, I do not fear to assert, might be regarded as the equals of the best soldiers in the world.

On the evening after this battle the exhausted enemy retired to appear no more, and the army of the Potomac took up a position and sought rest at Harrison's Bar, a spot chosen by the engineers and the navy as the most favorable for defence and for receiving supplies. The campaign against Richmond had ended, without success, but not without honor. The honor of the army was safe; but those who had looked to success for the early restoration of the Union under an impulse of generous and patriotic conciliation saw their hopes unhappily fade away.

VI.

Political Reflections.

Here I pause. My object in this narrative has been to describe the character of an American army, to make my readers acquainted with the peculiarities of war in countries so different from our own, and with the varied difficulties against which a general has there to contend. I have related with equal candor my good and my bad impressions. The good which I have seen there has often moved me to admiration; the evil has never weakened the sentiments of deep sympathy which I feel for the American people. I have also tried to lay my finger upon the sad concatenation of blunders and accidents which has brought about the failure of the great attempt made to re-establish the Union. I shall not venture to question the future upon the consequences of this failure. They will come to light only too soon. It would be idle and ridiculous to predict to-day the final destiny of the combatants, to foretell which of the two will display the greatest tenacity, will prove itself, if I may be pardoned the phrase, to have the better wind.

One thing is certain; the failure of McClellan's campaign against Richmond is destined to be followed by the effusion of seas of blood: it prolongs a strife, the fatal effects of which are not felt in America alone; it adjourns the most desirable solution of the crisis, the return of the States to the old Union. I say the old Union designedly, because I am one of those who think that if the North were beaten, decidedly beaten, that if the right of the minority to resist by arms the decisions of universal suffrage were victoriously established, the Union might still perhaps be reëstablished. But it would then be reëstablished by the conspicuous triumph of Slavery.

If the federal bond were to be finally broken between the North and the South, it would soon be broken, also, between the States which form the Northern Union. Each one of them would then consider only its own interests, while the South would be more and more closely united by the powerful bond of Slavery. It would have shown how strong it is; would have acquired great prestige, and would exercise that power of attraction which always goes with success and with power.

Victorious, it would extend its grasp not only over the now contested States of Missouri, Kentucky, and Virginia; but over Maryland also. Baltimore would become the depot of all foreign commerce. The iron of England would then enter the heart of Pennsylvania. Who can say that this State, the population of which perhaps dislikes the negro at liberty as much as it does the negro in slavery, would not decide to make its peace with the powerful confederacy in return for the commercial protection which the confederacy would be only too glad to offer it? For the Southern States favor free trade only because it suits their immediate purpose. Once masters of the situation, they would become genuine Americans again. New York would follow the example of Pennsylvania. Commerce does not suit the people of the South. They need some one to look after their business. In all probability a similar movement would affect the Western States, all whose outlets would be in the hands of the confederates. The States of New England alone, where puritanism holds its sway, and slavery is sincerely hated, would remain isolated, and exist upon the products of their agriculture, and the resources called into being by the enterprise of their active and numerous maritime population. With the exception of six States then, and probably of California also, which, separated from the rest of the world, has altogether exceptional interests of her own, the old Union would be reconstructed. But the ideas of the

South would be in the ascendant. The glorification and extension of slavery would be the common watchword. Founded by force of arms, the confederation would be an essentially military power. The slave aristocracy would have gained its sway, would have tasted the intoxication of glory, and would no longer acknowledge any restraint. Conservative at home, but aggressive abroad, it would no longer be controlled by the cool and almost British good sense of the mercantile North. With the impulse given to commerce by the return of peace, and therewith consequent prosperity, the confederacy, constituted as I describe it, would become a formidable power, and those who desire to see, more than aught else, a powerful State in Northern America, might give it their sympathies, if it had any chances of permanency.

But here is the difficulty. You may do great things with Slavery: acquire fabulous wealth in a short time, as of old in St. Domingo; call a whole population under arms, while the blacks till the ground, and so sustain a disproportionate struggle such as we now see going on in Virginia: but these are transient efforts, and in the long run, slavery exhausts, ruins, and demoralizes all that it touches. Compare the destinies of two great neighboring cities, Louisville and Cincinnati: compare the fate of the first, notwithstanding its immense natural advantages, under the enervating influence of slavery, with the development which its rival owes to Liberty. The fate of Louisville would be that of a Slaveholding Union.

The old Union, on the contrary, with its slow and prudent, but certain advance towards gradual emancipation, would have resembled Cincinnati. The old Union was a mercantile nation, furnishing Europe with the raw materials indispensable to her industry and offering her an unlimited market for her productions. This nation was useful to all the world, and whatever appearances may have been, it was not at bottom hostile to anybody.

The new Union would be military and aggressive, a condition of things favorable to some Powers, but unfavorable to others: the first was liberal and pacific; the second would have no other spirit of progress, no other system of assimilation than the spirit of war and the system of conquest.

Such, we think, would be the results of a Southern triumph. If on the other hand the conflict is to be prolonged, if the solution of this great debate is still to be delayed, then we must look for mischief of another sort. Urged by the passions and the pressure of the contest, the federal government may perhaps decree the immediate abolition of slavery, and may even be driven to the terrible resort of arming the slaves against their masters; but this measure, independently of its barbarity and violence, would be of no use to those who should adopt it. It would bring on in the North itself formidable dissensions more likely to help than to harm the cause of the Secessionists.

Need I add, that in the future seen under the aspect I have sketched, there is nothing which can meet the wishes of the friends of American liberty and greatness? When the blockade of the Southern coast had become complete, when the whole course of the Mississippi had fallen into the power of the federal navy, those friends longed for the triumph of the Army of the Potomac before Richmond, because it would have facilitated a complete reconciliation on the basis of the old Union. This triumph was not achieved; we have seen why; and reconciliation such as then was desirable and possible, seems very different to-day. Yet I am not one of those who will thence infer that the federal cause is lost. Compared to those of the South, the resources of the North are far from being exhausted; and who knows all that in a day of peril can be done by the energy of a free people, battling for the right and for humanity?

APPENDIX.

Note A.—Page 8.

Page 8.

MILITARY PREPARATIONS OF THE SOUTH.

The author here repeats in his estimate of the advantages with which the insurgent South began the war, an impression so general at the North that it may be considered to have become almost an article of faith, yet which I am constrained to believe erroneous. The "permanent militia" of the South here alluded to existed only upon paper, like the similar militia of the North. There were, it is true, in two or three of the States, and particularly in South Carolina and in Virginia, small bodies of troops maintained at the public expense for the protection of important arsenals or other public works, but these were insignificant in point of numbers. The "State Guard" of Virginia numbered not more, I think, than forty men, whose chief duty was to sentinel the Richmond Penitentiary and to inspect the statue of Henry Clay on the Capitol Square. The organization of the Southern militia was very far from deserving the encomium here passed upon it. It was in truth far inferior to the organization of the militia in certain States of the North, and particularly in Massachusetts and New York. The regimental organization which had been carried to such a respectable point of development in New York was almost unknown in the South. A few independent companies like the "Blues" of Richmond and Savannah, the "Washington Light Infantry" of Charleston, the "Washington Artillery" of New Orleans, and the "Richmond Howitzers" were as far advanced perhaps towards an adequate preparation for actual service when the war broke out, as any other militia companies in the country; but it is certain that in the whole South there were not so many well-drilled, uniformed, and efficient companies capable of acting together, regimentally, as would have sufficed to put a regiment at once on a war footing. The Seventh and the Seventy-first regiments of New York State Militia were bodies of men not to be matched in the South.

The military schools of Virginia and of South Carolina had no doubt educated a certain number of young men in the course of the last ten years to a higher degree of preparation for the duties of officers in the field than was brought to the service of the nation by the average volunteer officers of the armies first raised in the north; and I believe there is no doubt that Mr. Davis, Mr. Floyd, and particularly Mr. Henry A. Wise, did a great deal during the four years from 1856 to 1860 towards accustoming the Southern people to the idea of a more extensive military system than their manner of life and the geographical conditions of the country had previously encouraged. The "John Brown raid" contributed powerfully to the success of these efforts.

But the first armies called into the field by the South were quite as unmilitary in organization and not so military in appearance as their contemporaries at the North. The contrast between the bearing and equipment of the troops from Massachusetts, Vermont and New York, which I saw pass through New York in the Spring of 1861, on their way to Washington, and the army of General Johnston which I saw at Harper's Ferry in June of that year, might almost have excused the hasty self-confidence with which the North rushed into the operation of "crushing out the rebellion."

The author is equally at fault in his further discussion of this subject when he attributes to Mr. Davis the merit of having solidified the southern army by his judicious appointments of officers. In point of fact the nomination of the line officers of the southern volunteer forces which still constitute the great bulk of the southern army is not, and never has been in the hands of Mr. Davis. These officers are elected by their men; and it was a fact notorious in Richmond at the time of the battle of Fair Oaks that the chaotic condition into which the southern army fell, during that fight and particularly after the fall of General Johnston, was mainly attributable to the fact that in re-organizing the army in April and May, a vast proportion of the best officers of the line had been thrown out of commission in favor of others who had courted popularity by arts un-military, and who were wholly incompetent to the management of their troops. "Hierarchy and discipline" are things of very recent growth in the southern army. I have heard it stated, upon respectable authority in Virginia, that at the battle of Bull Run, in July, 1861, whole battalions of southern troops deliberately marched out of the fight, precisely as the author describes some of Fitz-John Porter's regiments to have done at the battle of Gaines's Mills.

Mr. Davis attempted, indeed, very early in the war to assume a general authority over the troops of the States. But he was met at the outset by the State authorities. At the head-quarters of General Johnston, to which I made a short visit in June, 1861, I saw for myself the difficulties thrown in the way of the confederate commanders, by the impossibility of their doing precisely what the author commends them for doing. In Georgia, the issue between the confederate and state organizations was made very early and very decisively by Governor Brown. Colonel Bartow, (afterwards killed at Bull Run,) having received a confederate commission and raised a regiment of men, applied to the state for arms. These the Governor refused to supply, declaring that Georgia should arm no troops whom she did not commission and organize. He should not prevent Bartow from going to Virginia, with as many men as chose to follow him, and when they reached Virginia, if anybody would give them arms they might form themselves into a regiment. But they would not be Georgian troops, and Georgia knew nothing about them. Colonel Bartow, raised quite a controversy over this matter, but the Governor was sustained by the people, and Bartow's men (who by the way followed him gallantly on the field of Manassas) were known as the "Independent regiment."

Note B.—Page 9.

FLOYD AND THE SOUTH.

THE Prince's charge against Mr. Buchanan's too famous Secretary, that he sent "all the contents of the federal arsenals to the South," is a clean case of *crescit eundo.* If the South had no positions more defensible than the character of Mr. Floyd, its conquest would indeed be easy: but that is no excuse for extravagant misrepresentations, which, if they have any force at all, only help to relieve us of responsibilities which we ought to accept. That Floyd would have been only too glad to send all the arms, and all the arsenals, too, of the country to the South, is doubtless true, but there were obstacles in the way of either operation, and it has never yet been clearly proved that he deprived any Northern State of her just quota of arms to the advantage of any Southern State. Indeed, he is blamed at the South for not doing what he is blamed at the North for doing; the simple fact being that he could not possibly do it. It was no doubt the opportunity and not the will which he lacked. For I remember that at Washington, in the winter of 1860–61, just before Floyd went to Virginia, he did his best to persuade certain southern leaders into a plan for a rising in Washington, or failing in that, for the seizure and removal to the South of General Scott. He was excessively disgusted at his inability to accomplish an organization for either purpose.

President Davis, who detests Mr. Floyd, seized upon his conduct at the surrender of Fort Donelson as a good occasion for disgracing him, and ordered him into arrest. He remained for some time at his home in Western Virginia, his particular organ, the "Richmond Examiner," meanwhile grinding forth, almost daily, imprecations upon the confederate government for its neglect of the "great soldier who had kept Rosecrans chained to the Gauley," and the "great statesman who had first warned the South to expect nothing from false and selfish England." The Legislature of the State was finally dragooned into providing for him. Authority was given him through the Governor, to raise ten thousand men, and he was commissioned a Major-General of Virginia. Whether he ever raised the men or not, I do not know. He had not done so three months ago.

I mention these circumstances, because I observe that the "Richmond Examiner" is constantly quoted at the North, as the representative of southern sentiment in general, whereas it is a fact notorious in Richmond, and indeed self-evident to any person whose unfortunate destiny has ever put him in the way of a prolonged familiarity with southern journalism, that the "Examiner" is simply the mouth-piece of Mr. Floyd's disappointed ambitions, political, military and diplomatic.

Note C.—Page 27.

THE EVACUATION OF MANASSAS.

I HAVE reason to believe that when the history of the present war shall come to be written fairly and in full, it will be found that General Johnston never intended to hold Manassas and Centreville against any serious attack; that his army at these points had suffered greatly during the autumn and winter of 1861–2; that from October to March, he never had an effective force of more than 40,000 men under his orders; that his preparations for an evacuation were begun as early as October, 1861, and that after that time he lay there simply in observation.

It was the opinion of accomplished officers of the southern army, that the reduction of Richmond would never be really attempted excepting by the valley of the Shenandoah, in a campaign intended to cut off the capital and the army from their connections with the west by the James river canal, and the Virginia, and Tennessee railways; or by the James and York rivers, in precisely such a movement as that which the Prince de Joinville states that it was the intention of General McClellan to make, had not his plans been disconcerted by the untimely and unnecessary revelation of them to which the Prince so delicately but so distinctly alludes. General D. H. Hill expected the campaign of the Shenandoah, but, it is my impression that the majority of the confederate commanders looked with more anxiety for the final advance of McClellan in the direction which it now appears that it was his intention to follow. The confederate government, however, scarcely anticipated any serious campaign from either quarter, and amused with dreams of an early peace through the influence of European intervention and of politico-financial causes at the North, kept Johnston's army in a position of observation on the Potomac, and utterly neglected all adequate preparations against such an expedition as the Prince relates General McClellan to have been silently preparing during the winter of 1861–2. There can be little doubt that the completion of the Merrimac in time to close the James river against our fleets, was quite as much a matter of chance as of design; the Secretary of the confederate navy having small faith in the work, and the people at large no faith at all. My own impression is, that the movement of General McClellan's army from its demonstrations along the Potomac to the base upon the James, selected for its operations against Richmond, could it have been put into execution as the author planned it, might well have proved so eminently and brilliantly successful, as to take its place in military history with such openings of a campaign, as Moreau's passage of the Rhine in 1800, and the Marshal de Saxe's sudden and magnificent transition from the demonstrations against Antwerp to the operations against Maestricht, in the Flemish campaign of 1748.

Note D.—Page 59.

CENSORSHIP OF THE SOUTHERN PRESS.

THE Prince only echoes a belief very general at the North, when he speaks of the "Complete Censorship of the Southern Press," but this belief is certainly unfounded. It is a curious trait of the existing war that every attempt on the part of the Richmond government to exercise a centralized control over the institutions of the different seceded States has been instantly, and so far as I know, successfully repelled by public sentiment. Reporters for the press were excluded from the lines of the Southern armies in the field early in the current year, but this was a military measure, and was acquiesced in as such. A tacit agreement subsequently grew up between the War Department and the Press that great reticence should be observed in regard to military movements. But a proposition to establish a formal censorship, made in January or February, 1861, was instantly sneered and shouted down throughout the South, and when, not very long afterwards, the commander of the department of Henrico, Brigadier-General Winder, permitted himself to threaten certain papers in Richmond with "suppression," he was met with open and contemptuous defiance; and very promptly modified his pretensions with no unnecessary delay. Whatever "censorship" exists at all in the South is a censorship of passion and not of power.

Note E.—Page 63.

RESPECT FOR SOUTHERN PROPERTY.

It is equally astonishing and unfortunate that the policy of forbearance in respect to the property and the persons of non-combatants in Virginia should ever have been the subject of unfavorable discussion in Congress. Aside from the abstract question involved, and from the moral influence of our practice in this particular upon the opinion of the world, it was only necessary to read the Richmond papers to perceive how anxiously the southern leaders desired to see us concede that disgraceful license of plunder and cruelty to the whole army which certain general officers of the army of the Potomac are alleged to have put to profit, until the practice was prevented by peremptory orders from the General-in-Chief. Confederate officers, who served in Western Virginia, at the beginning of the war, testified strongly, in my hearing, to the "bad effect" upon their men of General McClellan's forbearance and kindness towards the prisoners whom he paroled after the defeat of General Garnett. Every instance of pillage which occurred during the subsequent invasions in Virginia was sedulously magnified and published throughout the South. The result of all this was two-fold; it produced upon the soldiers in the field precisely the effect which Lord Dunmore aimed at in the early days of the Revolution, when he made the royal troops believe that they would be scalped if they fell alive into the hands of the "shirtmen;" and it so influenced the passions of the people against the northern "Hessians" as cruelly to increase the sufferings of our prisoners. I have seen the soldiers of the guard forced to protect prisoners in Richmond from the insults and violence of the citizens, and it was notorious that any official attempt to treat the federal captives decently would be universally denounced as soon as it was made public. General Lee himself was insulted in one of the Richmond papers, because his wife had accepted the protection of General McClellan for her household and herself.

Let me add that the private testimony of refugees in Richmond was almost unanimous as to the general good conduct of our troops, but this was as carefully suppressed, as was concurrent testimony of the same kind to the damage inflicted upon the country people by their southern "defenders,"

Whatever the issue of the pending struggle may be, we ought to remember that pillage in war is after all simply open robbery. Probably none of us would take any particular pride in calling the attention of his guests to a silver teapot stolen by his grandfather from a farm-house during the invasion of Canada; and we may surely do our posterity the trivial justice to believe that their respect for their ancestors will not be diminished by any display on our part of self-command, dignity, and reverence for those "holy bounds" of which Schiller sings so earnestly in his Wallenstein.

Note F.—Page 65.

OPENING OF JAMES RIVER.

The author speaks of James river as "opened to the federal navy" by the destruction of the Merrimac. This is perfectly correct; but it may be observed that James river was never closed to the federal navy till the Merrimac had been launched, proved and found far from wanting. The memorable panic occasioned in Richmond in April, 1861, by the news that the "Pawnee" was coming up the river, might have been supposed likely to point out to our own Government the wisdom of trying the experiment of a naval excursion from Fortress Monroe to Rocketts; and to the confederates the propriety of fortifying the river banks. It produced neither the one nor the other effect.

A couple of war steamers sent up the James when the army of McDowell advanced from Washington, might have neutralized the southern victory at Bull Run; and I have the authority of a southern naval officer for saying that the banks of the James were never adequately protected against the passage of even a single powerful gunboat until the works at Drewry's Bluff were extemporized in May, 1862. These works were thrown up so hastily, and so little was known or believed at Richmond of their capacity to resist a serious attack, that the excitement which reigned throughout the city during the dull gray morning of the day in which the heavy guns of the attack and defence were heard sullenly booming down the river, more nearly approached a panic than anything else which I witnessed during the whole time of my detention there.

The preparations of the governments, state and confederate, for evacuating the city had been hurried forward with great earnestness from the time when the sacrifice of Norfolk and the Merrimac became a probable military necessity; but there was such a conflict of councils in both governments that the successful passage of Drewry's Bluff would unquestionably have brought on a tremendous general catastrophe.

Note G.—Page 67.

"THE PARTISAN JACKSON."

It is singular enough that so many even of those who ought to be well informed in respect to the history and present position of the southern leaders should persist in writing and talking of "Stonewall Jackson" as a "partisan." He is scarcely a "partisan," even in the political sense of that word, for he was by no means a Secessionist in his convictions or his sympathies, and only joined the southern forces in the field, as I have been informed upon very respectable authority, from a religious sense of duty to his native State. I do not know that it is a greater stretch of charity to concede the possible existence of an honest "rebel" than of an honest atheist, and if Stonewall Jackson may be supposed to be honest, he belongs to the not inconsiderable class of men in the South who would draw the sword at the behest of their State as readily against the government of Jefferson Davis as against that of Abraham Lincoln. A partisan, in the military sense, Jackson has never been. He was graduated at West Point with the class of 1842, served with distinction in Mexico, and holds the rank of Major-General in the regular army of the "Confederate States." The partisan service has not been popular in the South, and most of those leaders who won their first spurs as partisans in Kentucky and Virginia have passed into the regular service as fast as they could find or make room for themselves. Turner Ashby was a confederate brigadier when he fell in battle, and John Morgan now holds that rank, his second in command being an experienced English officer, Colonel George St. Leger Grenfell, who resigned his Queen's commission and left a lucrative post in India, came from Calcutta to Havana, and "ran the blockade" into Charleston to put his sword at the service of the South.

Note H.—Page 68.

McDOWELL'S RECALL FROM FREDERICKSBURG.

The failure of the armies of McDowell and McClellan to unite before Richmond surprised the confederate commanders in the latter city more, I think, than any one incident of the war. They had endeavored, of course, to bring it about though I have some reason to doubt whether it was the primary object or expectation of "Stonewall" Jackson in his dashing Potomac campaign to effect this result. But it was not believed possible in Richmond for some days after it had demonstrably occurred. The cannon of Fitz-John Porter in the battle at Hanover Court House had sounded the knell of Richmond in the ears of those who knew the relative positions of the two federal armies. I was at that time living in a house on the extreme verge of Shockoe Hill, overlooking the line of the Virginia Central Railway, and on the 27th of May I received a visit from an European officer of distinction, then in Richmond, who brought me the news of what was going on, and said to me, "You will have the first view of the Yankees —they will march in on yonder lines;" pointing to the roads which wound away from beyond the crest to our left in the direction of Hanover Court House and Ashland. At that time the foreign consuls in Richmond had made all necessary arrangements for protecting the property of their fellow subjects; and almost every body who owned any tobacco or flour was eager to shift it, in one way or another, to the account of foreign owners. The fall of the city was considered inevitable.

Note I.—Page 72.

FAIR OAKS.

THE Prince's account of the condition of the confederates on the morning of June 1st, rather under than overstates the case. They were in a perfect chaos of brigades and regiments. The roads into Richmond were literally crowded with stragglers, some throwing away their guns, some breaking them on the trees—all with the same story, that their regiments had been "cut to pieces"—that the "Yankees were swarming on the Chickahominy like bees," and "fighting like devils." In two days of the succeeding week the provost-marshal's guard collected between 4,000 and 5,000 stragglers and sent them into camp. What had become of the command of the army no one knew. By some persons it was reported that Major-General Gustavus W. Smith had succeeded Johnston, by others, that President Davis in person had taken the reins of the army. General Johnston himself was supposed to be either actually dead or dying. He had been twice hit before he received the final wound which struck him from his horse. In falling he had broken two of his ribs, was picked up senseless and covered with blood, put into a hackney coach and driven to a house on Church Hill, where he lay between life and death for several weeks. The roads in the vicinity were covered with tan and all traffic interrupted by chains stretched across them near the house which he occupied.

Had I been aware on that day of the actual state of things upon the field, I might easily have driven in a carriage through the confederate lines directly into our own camps. It was not indeed till several days after the battle that anything like military order was restored throughout the confederate positions, or the last of the wounded brought in from the recesses of the woods and the intricacies of the secluded pathways in which they had lain dying a hundred deaths within four or five miles of the city and its hospitals. It is impossible to exaggerate the difficulties attending a general action in such a country. One gentleman who distinguished himself by his assiduity in seeking and bringing in the wounded from the field, told me that on three different occasions, within as many days, he had been forced to pass by wounded men, his carriage being absolutely filled and he walking by its side, that on each occasion he had noted as well as he could the position of the sufferers, and that on each occasion when he returned to seek for them he was compelled to give up the search in despair, so absolutely impossible was it to identify particular paths in that labyrinth of swamps and trees.

I do not think the Prince exaggerates the losses of the enemy in this sanguinary flight. There were published in the Richmond papers, detailed brigade and regimental reports of the losses in sixty out of seventy-two organizations, regiments, battalions and companies mentioned as taking part in the engagements. I computed these losses as they were published. The sum total was 6,732 killed, wounded and missing. The "Richmond Enquirer" nevertheless, which had published these very lists, relying I suppose upon the arithmetical indolence of its readers, coolly announced the entire loss of the confederates on the 31st May and 1st June to have been but 2,300 men! The official report was about 4,300.

As to the rain storm of May 30th, the Prince may well speak of it as "terrible." Never, even in the tropics, have I seen a more sudden and sweeping deluge. The creek which flowed at the bottom of the hill below the house in which I lived, and over which in ordinary times, a boy might easily leap, filled the valley on the morning of May 31st, with a shallow lake more than 100 yards in width.

Many confederate officers consoled themselves for the results of the battle of Fair Oaks, or Seven Pines as it is called at the South, by the consideration that in wounding General Johnston, and so compelling Mr. Davis to allow the command of the main army in the field to devolve upon General Lee, the federals had rendered them a great service. This was because the southern army under Johnston, was known to be suffering severely in numbers and *morale* from the same laxity in organization for which the Prince, in so friendly a spirit, finds fault with our own forces. Lee was considered, I should say, to have more of the talent essential for organization than any man in the service of the South.

NOTE K.—Page 85.

THE SEVEN DAYS' BATTLES.

The phases of public feeling and of military opinion in Richmond during the progress of the operation by which General McClellan transferred his army from the Chickahominy to the James, were highly interesting to me at the time, and it may be worth while for me briefly to describe them now.

Let me premise by stating however, that the Prince is certainly in error, when he speaks of General Beauregard as "lending the assistance of his capacity and his prestige" to the Southern army at this critical moment. General Beauregard was then at Eufaula, in Alabama, recruiting his health, shattered by two arduous campaigns, one in the East and one in the West. Very few, if any of the troops from his army were in Virginia. Reinforcements had been coming into the city for several days previously to the 25th, in very considerable numbers, but they appeared to me to be mainly made up of new troops, and were generally understood to be so.

Of the battle with Hooker on the 25th, in which the confederates were defeated, nothing was heard in Richmond save the sound of the cannonade, and to that we had all become so much accustomed as not to be much excited thereby. The negroes, who always, by some mysterious system of communication with the surrounding country, contrived to have news in advance of the published accounts, and whose reports I generally found to be quite as accurate as those of the "Dispatch" and the "Examiner," whispered indeed on the morning of the 26th in the servants' halls, from which the story soon ran up stairs, that something not altogether agreeable had happened the day before. But the popular rumor was, that a slight skirmish had taken place, with the inevitable result of "skedaddled" and captured Yankees.

About eight o'clock on the evening of the next day, the 26th, when after four hours of the nearest and most vivid firing, both with great guns and musketry that had yet been heard, the white wreaths of the curling cannon-smoke began to be drifted by the wind up the Shockoe valley into the heart of the city, and the smell of the gun-powder could be plainly perceived in Capitol Square, affairs took a more serious turn. I witnessed the fight of this evening myself from a favorable position on the outskirts of the city. I saw the confederate lines recoil, and our own artillery advance until between eight and nine o'clock. I began to think that we had really reached the crisis of the siege, and that Richmond was on the point of falling into the hands of the army of the Union. A young officer of artillery, a West Pointer from the old army, and belonging then to a detached corps of the C. S. A., who joined me in my post of observation about that time, and recognized with me the fact that the confederates were fighting on a line considerably in the rear of the positions which they had held about four P. M., borrowed my glass, looked long and earnestly through the deepening twilight on the scene before us, and then, turning to me, said in a hurried way,—"they will certainly be here to-night," and then, half laughing with an air of somewhat affected indifference added, as he tapped his light grey uniform coat, "had n't I better take this off and 'skedaddle' to Danville?"

By nine o'clock, however, and, so far as we could see, with no change in the relative strength of the firing on either side, the federal artillery still maintaining its plain and tremendous preponderance—the line of the federal fire began to recede. By half-past nine the affair was over, and after an hour or two of spasmodic and still receding discharges, mainly of shell, which burned in magnificent curves against the darkening sky, everything was once more quiet.

The next day was an anxious one to the people of Richmond. It was evident now that a general action was either imminent or actually in progress. The stories from the battle field of Gaines's Mill came in, announcing a great victory, and anxiety gradually turned into exultation, which grew as the prisoners began to arrive in small squads, and the people became convinced that the army of McClellan was actually retreating.

For the next day or two, this mood was in the ascendant, and nothing was talked of but the capture or annihilation of the whole "invading horde." Much was made of the two captured Generals Reynolds and McCall, who naturally grew into four, five or six, according to the strength of the speaker's patriotism, and of his imagination. General McClellan was killed three or four times, and General Sumner was certainly wounded and a prisoner at Savage's station.

Jackson's corps, which had not been engaged as the Prince seems to suppose on the 26th with McCall, the fight of that day being maintained on the confederate side by the troops of A. P. Hill and Longstreet in the advance, had come into action upon the federal retreat on the 28th, and this intelligence of itself would have sufficed to convince the most skeptical that the doom of the Yankees was sealed, and that the tobacco warehouses of Richmond would be too small to contain the prisoners that were about to arrive.

By the 30th, however, it began to be whispered that all was not going satisfactorily. It was then known to a few that McClellan had not been cut to pieces in detail; that on the contrary, he had succeeded in effecting the concentration of his whole army, and was moving on a line of retreat which, as it was not thoroughly understood, might perhaps, prove to be a new line of advance. The fearful tidings of the repulse and slaughter at Malvern Hill at last forced its way through the popular hope and passion, and the news that the gunboats in the river had joined their fire with that of the artillery of the federal land forces converted the rejoicings of the Virginians into doubts and disappointments. For some time it was supposed McClellan would resume his attack on the line of the Charles City road; then, that he would shift his whole force to the south side and throw himself irresistibly from City Point upon Petersburg. The results of the terrible six days' fighting were not regarded as at all decisive, and General Lee, while honored for his success in relieving the immediate pressure upon the city, and in "chastising the Yankees" tremendously, was loudly charged with having been outwitted by an adversary whose escape he ought to have rendered impossible.

The final movement which transferred the whole federal army from Harrison's Landing to the Potomac, and which was going on when I left Richmond was hardly credited at that time in that city. It was certainly felt that if real, it would be a substantial relief from all formidable operations against the place, at least for the next year.

As to the confederate forces engaged in these sanguinary battles before Richmond, it is my impression that the armies united under Lee before the arrival of Jackson from the Shenandoah, numbered 90,000 men; and the Prince's estimate of Jackson's force at 30,000, I take to be not far from the truth.

The prisoners taken from our army, including the wounded, whom we were forced to abandon, were estimated at between 7 and 8,000, of whom only about 4,500, however, were actually known to have been sent on to Richmond. On their own side, the most candid and best-informed confederates admitted a total loss in killed, wounded, and missing of about 16,000 men.

www.ingramcontent.com/pod-product-compliance
Lightning Source LLC
LaVergne TN
LVHW021424110826
845150LV00007B/2066

9781425508289